Restoring Worship

Restoring Worship

RECOVERING A FALLEN SOCIETY

LEE SHIPP

ISBN: 979-8-89694-658-8 - Ebook

ISBN: 979-8-89694-659-5 - Paperback

Table of Contents

The Value Of God's Presence

We can't blame God. If we were in God's place, we would have rained down wrath and judgment. We cannot stand to be mistreated. We would become furious if our mercy were thrown back into our faces. If we had just delivered a nation of enslaved people from four hundred years of servitude and abuse only to have them despise us and long to be enslaved again, we would not have offered to help them by giving them an angel (unless it were a fallen angel who would torment them.) But not God! He is not like us. He is kind. He is benevolent. He is gracious.

Why did it come to this? Why did God want to withdraw His presence and send an angel instead? What did Israel do? They forsook and blasphemed God! They created a golden calf; they got drunk; they took off their clothes and indulged in debauchery. Israel threw off all thoughts of the God who had delivered them and then danced around the golden calf, proclaiming that this was the god who delivered them from the house of bondage in Egypt. Honestly, what would you have done with such a people? The Lord wanted to give them an angel.

The Lord explained to Moses that if His presence went with Israel, He would destroy them because of their wickedness. But Moses interceded. Moses knew the name of God. He knew that God was merciful and gracious. He knew that the Lord was kind and forgiving. Moses appealed to God based on His divine nature. He interceded for the glory and reputation of God. Moses refused to go anywhere without the presence of God.

Now, wait before we think we would have acted as Moses did. How many of us would have chosen the angel? God promised the angel would guarantee five things:

1. He would give them entrance into the promise.

2. He would assure them of the entire inheritance of Abraham.

3. He would perform supernatural wonders and miracles.

4. He would deliver them from their enemies.

5. He would give them prosperity.

Would we be content with an angel? Would that be enough for us? I could only imagine the people responding to the Lord. "Really! Thank you, Lord. That is awesome. That would be so wonderful!" Imagine how excited many pastors and churches would be to have this promise of an angel who would give them miracles, deliver them from enemies, provide them with wealth, and fulfill promises! Imagine the evangelism! The people in church would be so excited. They would tell everybody at work and home in the neighborhood, "Oh, you just have to come to church; we have an angel there. You need to come and see this. He works miracles and fights for us." The church would be packed. After all, they can't say that about God … they rarely do. Many hardly ever get excited about church or God. Few ever invite their friends to come and see God. So, an angel would be a fantastic deal.

But not for Moses! And hopefully not for those reading this. Moses wanted God and would settle for nothing less. Praise God! Moses wanted the presence of the Lord. He knew there were things the angel could never give them. The angel could not give them rest. The angel could not provide them with grace. The angel could not make them holy. Only God can give rest, grace, and holiness. God's presence is proof that we have found grace with God. "And he said, My presence shall go with thee, and I will give thee rest. And he said unto him, If thy presence go not with me, carry us not up hence. For wherein shall it be known here that I and thy people have found grace in thy sight? Is it not in that thou goest with us? So shall we be separated (holy), I and thy people, from all the people that are upon the face of the earth" (Exodus 33:14–16).

I CHOOSE GOD

Moses knew it, and history proved it; nothing can take the place of the presence of God. Is Moses choosing an angel over God? I don't think so. I choose God. Just look what the Lord has done! What could compare to the Lord? Who could compare to the Lord? To whom would you liken Him? "Let

God arise, let His enemies be scattered ..." (Psalms 68:1). God rides upon the heavens. He is Father to the fatherless. He breaks the chains of those in bondage.

God went before Israel; look what happened in His presence: Sinai was moved, the earth shook, the heavens bowed, and the mountains trembled (Psalms 68). When Israel was brought out of her bondage, Judah was His sanctuary. Judah means praise. To this day, God inhabits praise. The sea saw Him and rolled up; the mountains moved. "What ailed thee, O thou sea, that thou fleddest? Thou Jordan, that thou wast driven back? Ye mountains, that ye skipped like rams; and ye little hills, like lambs? Tremble, thou earth, at the presence of the Lord, at the presence of the God of Jacob; which turned the rock into a standing water, the flint into a fountain of waters" (Psalms 114: 5–8).

What brought the water out of the rock? The presence of God. I cannot comprehend life without God's presence. "Whom have I in heaven but thee? And there is none upon earth that I desire beside thee. My flesh and my heart faileth: but God is the strength of my heart, and my portion forever ... it is good for me to draw near to God: I have put my trust in the Lord God ..." (Psalms 73:25–26, 28).

I celebrate David's song of rest. I have come to experience this life-saving truth. God is a safe place. God is my safe place, my hiding place.

> *The Lord is my light and my salvation; whom shall I fear? The Lord is the strength of my life; of whom shall I be afraid? When the wicked, even my enemies and my foes, came upon me to eat up my flesh, they stumbled and fell. Though an host*

should encamp against me, my heart shall not fear: though war should rise against me, in this will I be confident. One thing have I desired of the Lord, that will I seek after; that I may dwell in the house of the Lord all the days of my life, to behold the beauty of the Lord, and to enquire in His temple.

For in the time of trouble He shall hide me in his pavilion: in the secret of His tabernacle shall He hide me; He shall set me upon a rock. And now shall mine head be lifted up above mine enemies round about me: therefore will I offer in His tabernacle sacrifices of joy; I will sing, yea, I will sing praises unto the Lord.

Hear, O Lord, when I cry with my voice: have mercy also upon me, and answer me. When Thou sadist, Seek ye my face; my heart said unto Thee, Thy face, Lord, will I seek … When my father and my mother forsake me, the Lord will take me up … I had fainted, unless I had believed to see the goodness of the Lord in the land of the living. Wait on the Lord: be of good courage, and He shall strengthen thine heart: wait, I say, on the Lord. (Psalms 27)

DON'T LOOK FOR THE IMPOSSIBLE—LOOK FOR GOD

The impossible becomes possible in the presence of the Lord. You could tell when Jesus had passed through a Jewish village … there were no sick people left! Wherever He is, there are no problems with diseases, cancers, devils, storms, enemies, plagues, calamities, or grief. His presence is the answer to everything. It's just supernatural. Miracles happen in His presence. The elements bend to His will. There is no such word as impossible in God's dictionary. God's power, love, and goodness transcend all matter. God is not just supernatural. He is miraculous by nature. Everything about Him is miraculous, and so is everything He does.

Nothing shall be impossible if a man can but take hold of God. All Christians are not equal. Spirituality alone counts here; shut the door; no spectators are allowed; this is a secret place.

The reason many believers do not prevail is because of composure. Composure in the presence of God is foreign to princes with God: they cried, they prayed in tongues, they took hold of the invisible presence, and they conversed with the Someone no one else could hear.

What are we to do amid uncertainty? There is not much sense in counseling a Christian who has not prayed about their trouble. Who knows what God might do to help such people if they would only cry out? How often has someone spent time talking and worrying while the Lord of the universe waited to be invited into the fray? All they had to do was praise, but they would not.

THE ANSWER IS IN GOD'S PRESENCE

The presence of God is the difference. It is God's presence that brings transformation and joy. God desires the world to know those who have been in His presence. Moses was very concerned that he would not be taken seriously. Why would Egypt listen to his demand to let a nation of slaves go free? How could he prove God was sending him?

It mattered to God that Egypt and Israel knew Moses had been with God. So God had Moses surrender his rod, and that rod became the rod of God. Moses became the man of God. Why did this happen? Let the Lord tell us. God said to Moses, "That they may believe that the Lord God of their fathers, the God of Abraham, the God of Isaac, and the God of Jacob, hath appeared unto thee" (Exodus 4).

This is the essence of the church. This is the value of our life—we have been with God. There should be something supernatural about us. Our lives should be lived to make Jesus look great! We should not live as though Jesus is just a side interest. We should manifest to the watching world that our Jesus is the most exciting and worthy pursuit in all of life—that the joy of His presence transcends all other attainments. That is to say, heaven is only heaven because Jesus is there.

YOU NEED TO REST

Jesus has been everything to me. He has been my closest friend since I was a child. Everything I have, every hope I have, is because of Him. His presence is my rest. Beloved, we must learn to rest in the presence of the Lord, or the battle will wear us out. Prolonged hardships and relentless toil will allow the enemy to develop strategies for your destruction. The enemy will take the occasion of our weariness and emptiness to overwhelm us. No amount of sleep, nutrition, or entertainment can refresh a man from these conditions; only the presence of God; "My presence shall go with thee, and I will give thee rest" (Exodus 33:14).

But consider the successes of Satan against the saints, as so many are burdened with bitterness, depression, and fear. In every regard, the demands of a man's life are answered in the Lord's presence. The abusive effects of man's emotions are all tamed in the presence of God and excited to their proper function. It is here, in God's presence, where man can find an answer to his ANGER, INJUSTICE, BITTERNESS. Even the body is ministered to by God, for in the presence of God is healing. Have you ever prayed for God to give you a season of rest from the enemy? He will if you ask, even if amid a battle.

We must rest. At some point, a bowstring must be released, and the tension alleviated. Likewise, we must be released from the pressure. There are no tricks to this. There are no alternative solutions. In the presence of the Lord is rest. Our survival depends on His presence. I am not simply saying, "Take a break." I am not calling for a vacation. I am saying, "Retreat to our refuge. Be healed before our Father!" It is time that we are released from the enemies, the fear, the threats, the fighting, the strategies against us. I do not suppose these things disappear because we have God's presence. Oh no! David had God's presence, but he also fought many wars. Rest is not the absence of calamity, enemy attacks, or peril—rest is God's presence. Daniel was in the lion's den. What was he doing there? He was resting!

INTRODUCTION NOTES:

CHAPTER 1

Why Is The Culture Not Impacted By The Christian God

In his epistle to the Romans, Paul attributes the moral collapse of humanity to its refusal to worship God. Paul opens his letter to the Romans with a warning about neglecting God's worship. He concludes the same letter with a call to worship, begging the believers in Rome to worship God. It is amazing that Paul has to do this!

Both the ESV and Amplified Bible translations refer to worship as "spiritual" worship.

"I appeal to you therefore, brothers, by the mercies of God, to present your bodies as a living sacrifice, holy and acceptable to God, which is your spiritual worship" (Romans 12:1 ESV). The ERV adaptation calls it the "way" of worship. "So I beg you, brothers and sisters, because of the great mercy God has shown us, offer your lives as a living sacrifice to Him—an offering that is only for God and pleasing to Him. Considering what He has done, it is only right that you should worship Him in this way" (Romans 12:1 ERV). The CSB translation identifies worship as our "true" worship. "Therefore, brothers and sisters, in view of the mercies of God, I urge you to present your bodies as a living sacrifice, holy and pleasing to God; this is your true worship" (Romans 12:1 CSB).

In these scriptures, we see that the motivation for worship is the mercy God has shown to us. How tragic that Paul would have to beg believers to worship God. However, I find myself constantly having to beg believers to worship God as well. I honestly do not understand the callous neglect of our gracious Lord who has shown us such abundant mercy.

I also do not understand how many believers can withhold from God what is their spiritual worship, their way of worship, and their proper worship. This is all God has ever wanted from us, and yet those who are called by His name continue to draw near to Him with their lips, while their hearts are far from Him.

Is the lack of worship consequential? Absolutely. Paul shows that the failure to worship God appropriately will lead to the collapse of society. The reason for the cultural decay we see today is the lack of true worship, not the political maneuverings of Democrats and Republicans.

A great social confusion exists today: political confusion, gender confusion, moral confusion, educational confusion, and religious confusion (or might I say, perversion). There are four refusals Paul points to in explanation of this confusion and declension of society.

THE REFUSAL TO GLORIFY AND THANK GOD

Society's declension accompanies the refusal to glorify and thank God (Romans 1:21–22). This refusal is not from those who are lost but those who know God. This neglect of glorifying God (the ruin of praise) will lead to empty thoughts, tragic imaginations, depression, and hopelessness. It will lead to a gross deception of pride whereby one thinks himself to be wise when he actually is a fool. This is very prevalent in the church today.

The overwhelming majority of people in the church do not glorify and thank God. Look at the majority of worshipers in any given church during any given service; they are not praising God as the Bible instructs us. Yes, they have come to church. Yes, they draw near with their mouths, but their hearts are far from God. There is no passion, no animating love burning within the worshiping heart. The body is moving, but the heart is empty. It's no wonder that the number of depressed believers who need stimulants and drugs to cope is equal to the number of unbelievers taking these same drugs to deal with their depression. Paul said it would happen.

If believers do not glorify and thank God, they will think they know best when they don't know at all. They will be tormented with troubling thoughts and constantly battle depression. This refusal to glorify and thank God will lead to the second refusal, which will bring more significant consequences.

THE REFUSAL TO KEEP GOD HOLY

The continued downward declension will lead to the refusal to keep God holy (Romans 1:23–24). People will begin to think that God is like them. Have you ever heard someone say, "Well, if I were God …"? They are making God like themselves. This is the practice today. Many are comparing God to themselves. The tragic result of this comparison is the rise of immorality and homosexuality. Could sexual perversion possibly result from believers refusing to glorify and thank God? The Bible says that it does. A person who does not have lofty views of the Holy God will easily betray the image of God in man and pervert the natural use of man. Who is going to change the image of the incorruptible God but those who refuse to glorify and thank Him? It stands to reason that if one is willing to change the image of the incorruptible God, he will indeed have no problem degrading the image of God in man.

Anyone who cannot publicly demonstrate the worth of God is someone who has no understanding of His majestic glory. If one does not have a concept of God's holy worth, he cannot possibly esteem the value of the man made in God's image.

THE REFUSAL TO WORSHIP GOD

The downward spiral continues to the next stage of declension by refusing to worship God (Romans 1:25–27). Once man refuses to keep God holy, he will not keep God's Word holy. If believers can change who God is, they will change what God says. They will twist God's truth to accommodate their perversions and lusts. Instead of worshiping God, they will worship themselves.

Many leading denominations today are bowing to the woke culture; they are changing God's truth into a lie. Many churches and preachers today are too ashamed of God's truth to preach it, lest they offend.

The consequences of this are tragic. God gives them up. What else is He to do? They refuse to glorify and thank Him. They think they are wise and they have forgotten His holiness. They have changed His truth into a lie, so God gives them up; God gives them up to vile affections of homosexuality with the added consequence of incurable diseases. Is this not a pandemic problem in our world today?

THE REFUSAL TO THINK ABOUT GOD

Consequently, the next step of declension expresses itself in the fourth refusal, the refusal to think about God (Romans 1:28–31). How could the people mentioned above, who worship self, even want to think about God? They have so offended Him, turned from Him, and despised Him that the very thought of God is offensive (much less His truth or His worship).

All this confusion and perversion began with the simple refusal to glorify and thank God. This horrible treatment of God's person, God's truth, God's dignity, and God's rights has devastating consequences. People today do not want to feel accountable to God. Even to have a conversation about Him invites rejection.

People think they are wiser than God; therefore, why even bring Him up in a conversation unless it is to curse Him? The tragic results follow: God hands them over to a reprobate mind. Men begin to practice all sorts of lewd behaviors filled with sin, greed, and hatred. They have an insatiable appetite for murder, fighting, lying, and assuming the worst about other people. They gossip. They slander. They are rude. They hate God. They are proud. They do not obey their parents. They do not keep their word. They are cruel and lack mercy.

Oh, that we had ears to hear what the Spirit is saying and eyes to see what is so clearly happening in our world! Such behavior describes our world today; it describes America. It all begins simply because people who know God refuse to glorify and thank Him.

THE TURNAROUND

Believer, you may try to get yourself off the hook by saying, "Well, I don't murder. I don't practice homosexuality." Paul has words for you. "Though they know God's righteous decree that those who practice such things deserve to die, they not only do them but give approval to those who practice them" (Romans 1:32 ESV). Maybe you don't actually do this, but you support and like to watch those that do. You approve by enjoying these behaviors as entertainment: movies, music, and books that exploit this God-dishonoring behavior.

Is it possible to turn this around—to save ourselves from this perverse way of life? Is it possible to lead multitudes of this generation out of such confusion and pandemic immorality and into truth? Yes, it is possible, if believers would once again glorify and thank God for who He is. If believers would lay down their pride, stop thinking they are wise, and realize they have been foolish to treat God the way He has been treated in our churches, then this turnaround could occur.

Is it that simple? Yes! 1 Corinthians 2 says the natural mind thinks the things of the Spirit are foolishness. Why? Because they are wise in their own eyes but fools in God's eyes. They cannot understand that the solution to social and moral confusion in the world would come by worshiping God the way He deserves to be worshiped. And thus, the dilemma will continue because men are too proud and proper in their own eyes to see their need for the Holy Spirit. Only the Spirit of God is the means, the power, and the revelation of true worship.

If we would come to Him the way He asks, if we would praise Him the way He asked, if we would worship Him the way He asked, then our minds and hearts would be filled with truth, light, joy, and hope. This revival in the church would bring change and rescue our culture.

CHAPTER NOTES:

CHAPTER 2

The Perils Of The Religious System

And early in the morning he came again into the temple, and all the people came unto him; and he sat down, and taught them

(JOHN 8:2).

J esus sat and talked to the crowds! Wow. Jesus would be hard-pressed to succeed in today's high-powered show of preachers. He sat and talked—no running, no jumping, no distractions! Why? Because He had something to say, He had something to give. His words were full of the Spirit and struck the heart of all who heard Him.

Preachers today love to talk. Their preachings are performances. They know how to move the people but don't have anything to say. Compare the typical message proclaimed by the famed preachers of today with the latest motivational speaker, and you would find they basically say the same thing.

The man who is brought in to stir up the sales team is not much different from the modern preacher. Preachers disguise their lack of intimacy with Jesus and unfamiliarity with His Word by smoke and mirrors—from their flesh, they rile up the listener's flesh with great drama. Jesus sat and talked to the crowds; now there's a novelty!

I'm so bored with the religious system. I'm so bored with the "entertainer" preachers—the show, the game. I'm so bored with hearing the same messages over and over again saying, "This is your year, this is your breakthrough, this is your season."

I want people to come to church looking for Jesus; when they get there, I want Jesus to be center stage. I long for the day when people come to our churches craving the presence of the Lord and not the celebrity preacher. I grieve over the place Jesus has been given in this drama that bears His name but promotes the people. This is the church age we were warned about. A Laodicean age where the people have so many goods that they don't need Jesus. Well, beloved, I simply say, "Jesus is it! Period." There is nothing else. There is no one else. No one else is great—only Jesus! There is not enough time to talk about anyone else. There is no other gospel to herald but His!

The danger facing the contemporary preacher is the mixing of Kingdom Dominion theology and amillennialism with conservative truths. These former theologies insist upon global dominion by the church for Jesus. They demand that believers should walk in victory over hell in such a way that they never have a problem—no trials, no setbacks, no weaknesses, no brokenness, and no suffering. They feel the humble, broken, suffering believer is the reason Jesus has not returned, and until believers realize "who WE are," we will continue to delay Jesus' return.

Many solid believers who once considered these claims to be heretical have recently incorporated these theologies into their messages. The spirit of antichrist has crept in. This is probably because the American preacher wants to preserve his way of life; therefore, he must preach and stir the people to believe they can take over the world for Christ. They can abolish the corruption of modern government despite the scriptures warning of perilous days to come. Jesus even warned that men will wax worse, and the love of many will grow cold.

THE FORM OF GODLINESS

Paul foresaw the church being overrun with godly performances but barren of actual power (2 Timothy 3). Sadly, these religious zealots we see today do not know they are without power; they do not know that the show, the riches, and the performances have pushed Jesus out. "We are rich and increased with goods," they say. "We have need of nothing," they say; all the while, Jesus is knocking on the door to be invited back in. They gauge their power based on their ability to prevail over the people, not their ability to prevail with God, as when Jacob became Israel.

The modern preacher would have us believe that the only thing America needs is a godly president to save the day. Please understand, I do believe in Christians running for office and making a positive difference in the world. I believe that the most valuable citizen of any country or local municipality is the church of Jesus Christ. I also believe in the preachers of truth who are excited and preach with vigor—running, shouting, jumping, and all sorts of other things. However, when that powerful church came out of the upper room and turned the world upside down, they did not convert Rome. Though multitudes would take refuge in the Kingdom of God, Rome would "bring the hammer down" on the church with swift and final persecution. Why do we think we shall escape persecution for the gospel's sake? This mixture of "Kingdom Now" theology has been added, and all stands to be lost. The reason is that many who put their faith in this system will eventually realize they have been sold a bill of goods that have no root in God's Word or gospel.

The preachers of this mixture dare to be confronted. They dare to be corrected. They refuse to even listen to a biblical question. They have dug their heels in and are not budging. They demand, "We are the ones. This is our day. We shall take over. We are the victors." However, they have no concept of what the victory of Jesus even entails or how it occurs. They deny brokenness, which is the only way to power. They deny weakness, which is how God's grace rests upon us (2 Corinthians 12:9). Paul gloried in his infirmity. Still, these modern preachers believe that if you have infirmity, you lack the understanding of who you are in Christ.

What is the motive for all this? It is Satan's new apple. Eat this "Christ," and "YOU" will become .... They are declaring things they are willingly ignorant of. They receive words, but they have not studied to show themselves approved. These modern preachers would renounce Paul because he confesses weakness and humility and is the worst of sinners; such humility is foreign to them. They would insinuate that Paul does not know who he is in Christ. They think he speaks too much about suffering and brokenness and displays no victory and power?

Recently, I was confronted by one of these preachers. He rebuked me because our church had several suffering people. Some of these battled sickness. Those condemning me were blind to the grace of God operating through the ministry He has given me—blind to the presence of God among us, the testimonies of miracles, the joy of God's presence, and the powerful salvation of people coming into the Kingdom of God. They could not even see they were suffering and sick, had been married multiple times, and watched their loved ones die from sicknesses.

Here are the words of Paul from 2 Corinthians 11. Paul tells the Corinthians it is a shame that he must defend his apostleship in Christ. But his life was under attack by false accusers, and Paul decided to act. He listed his credentials. Understand, these credentials are despised by this contemporary preaching machine today. Paul would explain, "You Corinthians love the men who exalt themselves over you, who control and put you under their spell." Furthermore, he too could boast of his lineage: being a Hebrew and a minister of Christ. But instead of boasting about what exalts him, he gives his testimony: I am exhausted from the work, beaten beyond measure, frequently in prison, dying constantly. I have been beaten with rods, once stoned, three times I suffered shipwreck. For a whole day and night, I floated in the ocean. I am frequently on the go, putting me in constant danger from robbers, my countrymen, and the heathens. I face perils in the city, wilderness, sea, and among false brothers. Shall I go on? Okay. I am weary and suffer much pain. I sleep very little. I am often hungry and thirsty. I suffer from exposure to nature, being both cold and naked. Wait, that's not all: every day, I am overwhelmed with the care of the churches. The modern preacher thinks, "Poor Paul; he just doesn't have much faith." Wait! Paul is not finished with his credentials: I am weak. I am offended!

Now, it is Paul's turn to tell you a thing or two about this life of Christ. Here it is, and I quote, "If I must needs glory, I will glory of the things which concern mine infirmities" (2 Corinthians 11:30). Wow, you do not hear preaching like this today!

Paul is not finished. He went on to say that God allowed a demon to hinder him! Oh my, preach that today! Paul said God explained it was to keep him humble. Again, the contemporary preacher would insist, "If Paul only knew who he was in Christ, he could have enjoyed such a greater victory."

Will the contemporary preacher teach Paul the right way to believe? I can imagine the contemporary preacher delivering his message of power and victory to Paul. Let him explain to Paul of his greatness. Let him explain to Paul that he should not confess weakness or defeat. He cannot suffer brokenness, for he is the head and not the tail; he holds the keys to the Kingdom; he is the power of God on earth. I could see them instructing Paul that his churches suffered division through satanic attack, sickness, and suffering due to Paul's ignorance to preach who they are in Christ.

PAUL GLORIED IN SUFFERING

Paul has an answer! Here it is, "Most gladly therefore will I rather glory in my infirmities, that the power of Christ may rest upon me. Therefore, I take pleasure in infirmities, reproaches, necessities, persecutions, distresses for Christ's sake: for when I am weak, then am I strong. I am become a fool in glorying; ye have compelled me: for I ought to have been commended of you: for in nothing am I behind the very chiefest apostles, though I be nothing" (2 Corinthians 12:9–11).

There it is; Paul says he is nothing. But the modern preacher, with his mixture of Kingdom Dominion theology, would rebuke Paul and say, "How can you say you are nothing? Do you not know who you are in Christ?" Furthermore, he cannot understand how anyone in Christ could celebrate infirmities, reproaches, lack, persecution, distress, and weaknesses; for he cannot comprehend how the grace of God works in a broken man.

Paul called this glorying! Amazing! Most today would call it defeatism. How could Paul take pleasure in these things? Because of the immeasurable grace of God that would rest upon him, giving him supernatural power and victory.

Paul had to comfort his friend Timothy regarding this suffering. In his second letter, Paul said, "Be not thou therefore ashamed of the testimony of our Lord, nor of me his prisoner: but be thou partaker of the afflictions of the gospel according to the power of God" (2 Timothy 1:8). Paul is exhorting ministers to take part in the afflictions; you don't hear preaching like this today.

He testified that he unashamedly suffered because he was a preacher! His confidence was in the world to come, not his acceptance in this world. In 2 Timothy 1:12 Paul declares, "For I know whom I have believed, and am persuaded that He is able to keep that which I have committed unto Him against that day."

Paul sought to encourage Timothy to remain strong, not to be weakened by Paul's afflictions; therefore, Paul assured Timothy of his calling by listing his credentials as God's minister. Paul explained to Timothy that he should be joined to Paul because he knew his doctrine, way of life, purpose, faith, patience, love, and self-control.

He unashamedly spoke of the persecution and afflictions he endured for the gospel: but the Lord delivered him from them all. He expressed to Timothy, "… all that will live godly in Christ Jesus shall suffer persecution. But evil men and seducers shall wax worse and worse, deceiving, and being deceived" (2 Timothy 3:12–13).

No doubt Timothy struggled with Paul's persecution. Obviously, Timothy was enticed to forsake Paul and join the ranks of those preachers who seemed to find the easy way of serving the gospel. Paul addressed these in 1 Corinthians 4. He said that God had exhibited the apostles as last and not first: like men sentenced to death, a spectacle to the world, to angels, and men. But other preachers, who thought they knew better than Paul, bragged about how wise they were in Christ. Paul said, "We are fools for Christ's sake, but you are wise … We are weak, but you are strong. You are held in honor, but we in disrepute." This sounds so familiar today.

What an embarrassment Paul must have been to so many in his day; no wonder Timothy suffered because of Paul's sufferings. Just look at Paul's life in Christ: "Even to this present hour we hunger and thirst, we are naked, and buffeted and with no certain dwelling place …" Hold on to your seats because Paul is about to make an incredible appeal, "I urge you, then, be imitators of me" (1 Corinthians 4:16 ESV). I assure you; this modern religious system will not follow Paul!

Today's modern orthodoxy runs counter to the scriptures and the testimony of Paul. Instead of encouragement in suffering, brokenness, and affliction, they exhort others much like Satan did Eve. They have a zeal but without knowledge.

It is all so dangerous—leading to such discouragement. These so-called followers are so consumed with their identity in Christ that they don't need Christ. They are so focused on what *I am* that they don't need the *I Am*. So much talk of *You* that they don't need *Him*. So much *anointing* that they have no intimacy with the Holy Ghost, so much mixture of *Kingdom Now* because they don't understand the Kingdom now. They are like the disciples when they cried to Jesus regarding the demon possessed child, "Why could not we cast him out?" (Matthew 17:19). What made the disciples think they could cast out a devil apart from Jesus, anyway? The same spirit invading the church today proclaims we can do all things because of who *WE ARE* in Christ but without Christ. This current charade has made Jesus the means to our greatness, just like Satan's apple to Eve. Jesus is not my *means* to greatness; He *is* my greatness. It is not what I am, but what Christ is—the hope of glory in me. I must decrease, and He must increase.

IF NOT NOW, WHEN?

Beloved, Jesus told us of the imposters coming who claim to be The Way. Paul warned of the doctrines of devils and seducing spirits coming in the last days. Jude called us to contend for the faith that was once delivered. Did Jesus, Paul, and Jude get it wrong? Do we have nothing to worry about regarding false teachers? Was Jesus being sarcastic when He asked if He would find faith on the earth when He returns?

If Jesus, Paul, and Jude were serious, the questions must be asked; Where are the false witnesses today? Are we to live thinking they are not around? Is it possible they are gaining momentum as we read this article?

Because such false witnesses don't understand the Kingdom of God, the coming of Christ, and victory through weakness, they rush into the world with half-truths of Kingdom theology only to get pulverized by the world system time and time again. To truly understand the life of Christ, Christ must be our life. We can do nothing without Jesus, but for them, this requires too much quiet time and intimacy of prayer. It simply requires too much time away from the stage for today's preacher.

Multitudes of true believers stand to suffer great trials of their faith as these preachers mix truths with lies. The people will see these doctrines do not fit reality. These errors could cause the believer to throw their confidence away. Constantly reminded of who they are in Christ but unaware of Christ, they will be swallowed up with confusing experiences; persecution will weaken their faith. They will not understand why sickness is not healed. They will even blame God for the triumph of evil and wicked men.

WE ARE MORE THAN CONQUERORS

We are victorious. We are more than conquerors through Him who loved us. God has anointed us with power and given us the authority to go into the world to make Him known. We have a treasure inside these earthen vessels to the end that the power may be of God, not us (2 Corinthians 4:7).

Paul said he was troubled on every side, but he was not distressed. He was perplexed but not in despair. He was persecuted, but not forsaken; cast down, but not destroyed (2 Corinthians 4:8–9). How? Why? I get it; I really do. How can a people in whom the power of God dwells, ever be perplexed, troubled, persecuted, and cast down? How can there be weakness? How can believers with the power of the Holy Spirit experience confusion? How can that be? I understand the reasoning, but reasoning will never answer these questions; only faith can answer the chaos of life. What is the victory? How is this power demonstrated? Why did Paul rejoice in his afflictions? The answer is this: the way to victory is the way of brokenness.

If the power of God, and the life of God, is to be manifested through the believer, then the believer has to be broken. For the life of Christ within us to come forth from us, we must be handed over to death. This is not for our defeat, but victory. This is the victory; the life of Jesus in us will defeat death. We must bear in our bodies the dying of Jesus so the life of Jesus can be seen in us. We are actually handed over to death for Jesus' sake (2 Corinthians 4:10). Why? So that the life of Jesus can be manifested in our mortal bodies.

Paul was not depressed by this calling of God. He rejoiced in his infirmity, for the grace and power of God rested upon him. Paul was satisfied with knowing that his suffering for Christ was supplying grace to the people and glory to God. It was a cause so noble he could not faint; it was too glorious (2 Corinthians 4:18). God renewed him every day by assuring Paul that his suffering was only for a brief moment; however, the glory would be far exceeding and weighty.

This modern spirit of preaching is pointing the believer to anything but Paul's teaching. What is the dangerous result? Our generation will not see Christ manifest through His church. If the life of Christ is manifested by the believer's suffering and the believer is taught not to suffer, then the generation will not see the life of Christ. If death cannot work in us, then how will the life of Christ work in you? (2 Corinthians 4:12).

Sadly, this cannot be preached in most circles today. The people cannot handle it. They reject that kind of Christianity. Modern preachers know this; therefore, they give the people what they want. They tell them about how great they are. They tell them all the good they are going to walk into. Paul said these preachers would come. "For the time will come when they will not endure sound doctrine; but after their own lusts shall they heap to themselves teachers, having itching ears; and they shall turn away *their* ears from the truth, and shall be turned unto fables" (2 Timothy 4:3–4).

Paul said in 2 Corinthians 4 that it is in death that Christ is revealed. If Christ is not revealed, the light goes out in the world. The contemporary preacher does not realize what he is producing when he elevates the people and diminishes Jesus, but Satan does. There is no death in modern evangelism. No brokenness. But still, the truth remains: victory always comes from the cross life.

The Father is not looking for preachers, teachers, evangelists, musicians, or praise teams. The Father is looking for worshipers; worshipers He can preach through, sing through, and teach through. Many have time to sing to God, but few are worshiping God.

Worshiping God is the surrender of our lives to drink God's cup for us. Jesus in the garden, faced with the bitter cup, drank it all for the Father. His suffering and death would bring an explosion of life and freedom into the world. Hell would be broken!

The Holy Ghost comes upon worshipers; He overshadows them and puts His life in them. Then He breaks them with such grace that the life of Jesus comes out into the world. The life of Jesus will come forth from you, affecting the nations.

Life defeats death, not theologies and doctrines, but Jesus. His life, His personality will dominate what is destroying this present world. The answer to everything in our lives (our families, our society, and our world) is that we could rejoice in suffering and be handed over to death, so the life of Christ can pour out. The answer to this world is "Who" lives inside us, not "what" we claim we are—not our confession, but our Christ!

CHAPTER NOTES:

CHAPTER 3

The Burning Heart
And The God Of Fire

T he Holy Spirit has been sent to us to give us the power to testify of Jesus, to speak of His kingdom, to see God, and to worship Him in spirit and in truth. History has recorded the power of those who were living sacrifices, those who gave God their worship and God gave them His fire. They were persecuted and threatened. They called prayer meetings and attended them. They prayed for the courage to continue to preach and then preached. God worked with them. He was there. The Spirit of God demonstrated the truth of their gospel with miracles. The world did not love them, but God did! Persecuted and suffering, they continued to worship the Lord as living sacrifices. The only explanation for such people was that they were Spirit-filled; their hearts ignited by the God of fire.

This burning heart continued until some theological smart man came along and suggested that their demonstration of

Jesus should be calmer. They need not present themselves to Jesus with such zeal. Instead, they suggested a way to live that would be more acceptable—a Christian lifestyle that was non-offensive to the world. These intellectuals removed believers from the altar of fire. They removed the passion. Tired of suffering and rejection, this new brand of disciple wanted the world to know they were its friends; they had come to help.

These disciples changed their worship from that which honored God to that which was non-offensive to the world. They exchanged the fire of God for the approval of the world. The Holy Spirit was sent to the corner lest He embarrass them. However, with Him went the miracles, the love, the glory, and the power.

The key to worship is not worship itself. There is not a lack of worship today. Worship is possibly the most popular behavior in the world. It is everywhere. Even among secular superstars, worship music is trendy. I do not demean modern worship or the incredible worship leaders writing beautiful songs to Jesus. Remember that Saul, filled with demons, desired the rest he got from David's worship. My point is this: there is not a lack of worship, but a lack of appropriate worship.

Romans 1 calls for God's worship, the kind that explodes with people glorifying and thanking Him. It is worship that magnifies God as incorruptible and holy and loves His truth; a truth that loves to think and speak about God all the time. This is worship—to love God. It is not to look for the way out or the easy path. It is to look for the path of sacrifice and love.

God wants us to be alive to Him, not dead. He wants our lives to count. God wants to baptize us in the Holy Ghost and fire. I have witnessed people who once benefitted from baptism in the Holy Ghost and fire only to reject this gift later. They were not rejecting a doctrine, but rejecting the person of the Holy Spirit. They were rejecting Jesus' baptism. Immediately, their lives changed. The fire went out in their anointing. They were calloused and hardened—lazy in their zeal for the Lord. Numbers of these would approach me, asking, "What happened to me? Something terrible has occurred."

We cannot offend the Holy Spirit and continue to live as usual. Once we have tasted this gift and walked in the power of this gift, we cannot simply say we no longer believe and avoid the consequences. Things will drastically change for the worst in our lives. We will lose our worship. We are not rejecting an event. We are not rejecting a doctrine. We are rejecting the person of the Holy Spirit and the work of Christ.

Without the Holy Spirit, we cannot worship God; without appropriate worship, we cannot recover the culture. The Father is looking for those worshiping Him in Spirit and Truth. Beloved, let your heart burn with the fire of the Spirit.

BELIEVERS NEED TO BE BAPTIZED IN THE HOLY SPIRIT

Why did the church see the necessity of sending Peter to Samaria? They sent him there so that the people would be able to receive the Holy Spirit, as they were already baptized in Jesus. According to Acts 8, here is how it all started: Philip preached Christ to Samaria, and the people responded. Great miracles occurred. Demons were cast out of people. The lame were healed. Those with paralysis were healed. Afterwards, the city was filled with great joy!

They believed Philip as he preached the things concerning the Kingdom of God and the name of Jesus Christ and were baptized (Acts 8:12). When the apostles in Jerusalem heard about the revival, they sent Peter and John so that the believers in Samaria would receive the Holy Ghost—for He had not fallen on any of them. They had only been baptized in the name of Jesus Christ. When Peter and John arrived at Samaria, they found the city and the believers in the state of salvation as it had been told to them; therefore, Peter and John laid their hands on the people, and they received the Holy Ghost (Acts 8:17).

The point of this story: people who put their faith in Jesus need to have the Holy Spirit fall on them; they must be baptized in the Holy Spirit. Faith is not academic; it is supernatural. To live a life worthy of God, that life must be filled with and led by the Holy Ghost. Jesus promised His followers that He would baptize them in the Holy Ghost and fire. This and nothing less is true worship. This is the presentation of our bodies to God as living sacrifices. Apart from the power of the Holy Spirit, how can we ever magnify the Lord as He deserves?

THE ANSWER TO THE CULTURE

If the collapse of the culture is due to believers failing to worship (Romans 1), then the deliverance of the culture comes in worshiping God. Often, many think worship involves music, notably slower-style songs. This is false. Romans 12 clearly shows that our true worship is to present our bodies as living sacrifices. God will receive this worship and manifest His power through these earthen vessels to recover what is His. This power is demonstrated through His gospel.

Men do not send believers into the harvest. Denominations do not send them into the harvest. The Lord of the harvest sends into the harvest. He will send only those who are filled with His precious Holy Spirit, even if the harvest rots.

"Therefore said he unto them, The harvest truly *is* great, but the laborers *are* few: pray ye therefore the Lord of the harvest, that he would send forth laborers into his harvest" (Luke 10:2).

Pray the Lord of the harvest to send forth laborers into the harvest. Though laborers are few, the prayer is not for increasing the number of laborers. The prayer is that the Lord would send the few forth!

Why would the Lord not send all the believers? For what reason would He not let others go? Without controversy, Jesus made it clear to His disciples that they were not to go forth into the world until they were endued with power (Acts 1). How could they go into a hostile world full of devils and ruthless men and effectively worship God without the power of the Holy Ghost? Jesus knew that without the Holy Spirit His disciples would never be able to worship God in the culture.

The tragedy of the church at the end of days is that men are content with a form of godliness; men not filled with the power of God. ***What good are our bodies, given to God in worship, if they have no power?*** Men who are not filled with the power of God have not the ability to worship. How can they bear God's excellent presence without the power of God? How can they walk with God apart from the Holy Spirit's power? That is why God is not sending forth some to labor. That is the reason many do not know their calling and election. That is why many do not move in the gifts—they have no power. If they have no ability, they have no worship.

God wants our lives to be worship to Him. It is the Spirit-filled life that magnifies the Lord: a life of ability and power, a life that is alive and sacrificed for the cause of Christ. That is what was seen in the upper room when Pentecost came—one hundred and twenty believers presenting their bodies to God and waiting for the Holy Ghost to give them power. The Spirit came, gave them power, and they went forth and turned the world upside down!

Was this the pattern? Did this continue beyond these eleven apostles? Yes! Paul claims to have received the same anointing as did the believers in Samaria. Furthermore, Paul declared that he had the ability to preach the gospel with power; he claimed that he had a "full gospel." This means that the gospel Paul preached included mighty demonstrations of the Holy Spirit. "Through mighty signs and wonders, by the power of the Spirit of God; so that from Jerusalem, and round about unto Illyricum, I have fully preached the gospel of Christ" (Romans 15:19).

The term "full gospel" means the gospel that is preached and demonstrated through mighty signs and wonders by the power of the Spirit of God. The life filled with the Spirit of God is the highest worship. Furthermore, the baptism of Jesus is promised to all who would believe in Jesus, "And it shall come to pass in the last days, saith God, I will pour out of my Spirit upon all flesh: and your sons and your daughters shall prophesy, and your young men shall see visions, and your old men shall dream dreams: and on my servants and on my handmaidens I will pour out in those days of my Spirit; and they shall prophesy: And I will shew wonders in heaven above, and signs in the earth beneath" (Acts 2:17–19).

DOES GOD NEED THE CHURCH TO ACCOMPLISH HIS WORK?

A question must be asked and settled. Does God need people to accomplish His work? According to the scriptures, the answer is yes! In 1 Corinthians 12, the Holy Spirit makes it very clear that for the body to be whole … all must function in their gift.

1 Corinthians 12 declares that the body is one. The body is composed of many parts; all the parts make ONE BODY. This is the body of Christ, the Church. Now, the Holy Spirit has placed a variety of gifts within the members of His body: there are different administrations; there are different operations and different manifestations of the Spirit, but all these functions are the result of the same Holy Spirit working in every man differently as He wills (1 Corinthians 12:4–12).

Does God need the individual believer to fulfill His will in the body? Absolutely. How can any individual deny this need for worship if they are a part of the whole? Remember that the whole needs what the Holy Spirit desires to work through each believer. "But the manifestation of the Spirit is given to every man to profit withal" (1 Corinthians 12:7). Without functioning in the Holy Spirit, the rest of the body cannot profit. The body needs what each has. Therefore, let us present our bodies as living sacrifices to the Holy Spirit. Let Him have His perfect work done through us. This is worship.

Tragically, most of the Pentecostal world is not Spirit-filled. They had an experience, but they have no worship. They can speak in tongues, but they have no power. It doesn't matter how their hand shakes when they pray; how they cry when they pray; how they preach; how they go to church and read their Bibles; how they are no longer "worldly"—I want to know how they love their enemies! I want to know how they are laying their lives down for those who abuse them!

Worship is not seen in what we don't do—that is *Pharisaism*. I want to know what we do. Do we have the power? Worship is life! Life is the New Covenant anointing. Do we have the ability that makes cities happy? Do we have the power to set people free from their bondage? Are we set free from our own bondages?

Two thousand years ago, a small group of unlearned men and women came out of an obscure room. They were filled with the Holy Spirit. They turned the world upside down. That is worship. They had burning hearts. They demonstrated a powerful love for God and others. Their shadow fell on the sick and demon-possessed, and they were set free. They spoke to kings. They defied governments. They raised the dead.

Today, our world needs these kinds of believers. The Holy Spirit needs these kinds of believers. Our songs do not matter if we are not worshiping God. Our preaching does not matter if we are not worshiping God. The demonic confusion of our day will not be corrected by polite talk. The raging fury that drives masses of people to burn down cities will not be quenched by apologetics. If preaching were the answer, America would have never turned as dark as it is today. Worship is missing. Fewer believers are presenting their bodies to God as living sacrifices. Beloved, restore God's worship, and you will see the change you have been praying for. You are not waiting on God to move; He is waiting on your worship.

CHAPTER NOTES:

CHAPTER 4

The Pathway to the Father

By love, through love, and for love, the Father gives. He gives His greatest. He gives His heart. He does not give His least. He does not give merely enough. He gives gratuitously. He gives without regard to the receivers' appreciation. He gives because of His love—unconditionally. The Father's giving is not based on the benefactor deserving His best, but because His love can only give the best. His giving is the manifestation of His loving. He is calculating and extravagant.

His great giving is not based on the benefactor receiving or understanding the priceless demonstrations of love. He simply gives His treasures because He loves. He loves completely and perfectly. He cannot love less. All He does is perfect. His loving is perfect. His loving is more than enough. Whether received or crucified He loves, and because He loves, He gives!

The Father does not give in stages. He does not give in degrees. His judgments are in degrees, but He does not love that way. He gives His love gifts to save what He loves. He provides it all so that the lifeline is complete and lacking nothing. The benefactors of His love will never be able to say that His love lacked. Forever, His love is wounded and scarred by those who hated His heart.

He is a Father to the fatherless and a champion of the widows. The Father sets the lonely in families; He breaks the chains of those in bondage. Our Father loads us with blessings: He forgives all our iniquities. He heals all our diseases. He redeems our life from destruction. He covers us with tender mercies so as not to crush us. He satisfies us. He is the merciful and gracious Father.

He is very gentle and slow to anger. He will not deal with us according to our sins. His mercy reaches into the heavens, and He has put our sins away as far as the east is from the west. He has a Father's pity toward us. He knows us: our frame, our days, our weaknesses, our tears, the hair upon our head.

Our Lord has no equal. No god is like Him. "Lift up your eyes on high, and behold who hath created these things, that bringeth out their host by number: he calleth them all by names by the greatness of his might, for that he is strong in power; not one faileth. There is none like ... God ... who rideth upon the heaven in thy help, and in his excellency on the sky. The eternal God is thy refuge, and underneath are the everlasting arms: and he shall thrust out the enemy from before thee; and shall say, Destroy them. Happy art thou ... O people saved by the LORD ..." (Deuteronomy 33:26–27, 29).

"Why sayest thou ... My way is hid from the LORD, and my judgment is passed over from my God? Hast thou not known? Hast thou not heard, that the everlasting God, the LORD, the Creator of the ends of the earth, fainteth not, neither is weary? There is no searching of his understanding. He giveth power to the faint; and to them that have no might he increaseth strength. Even the youths shall faint and be weary, and the young men shall utterly fall: but they that wait upon the LORD shall renew their strength; they shall mount up with wings as eagles; they shall run, and not be weary; and they shall walk, and not faint" (Isaiah 40 -27-31).

Our Father in heaven loves His enemies, blesses those who curse Him, and is good to those who hate him. Our Father in heaven is our provider relieving us from worrying about what we are to eat, drink, or wear. Our Father gives good things to His children. He seeks the worship of His children.

He is the God of all comfort, for He has adopted us as His children and begotten us again to a living hope by the resurrection of the dead—assuring us of an inheritance incorruptible, undefiled, that will not tarnish, and is waiting for us in heaven. Our Father will get us home.

He is the God of peace, and "Through the blood of the everlasting covenant He will make us perfect in every good work to do his will, working in us that which is well pleasing in his sight, through Jesus Christ; to whom be glory for ever and ever. Amen."

LONGING FOR THE FATHER

Jesus longed for the Father's presence. He had a habit of retreating to desolate places to commune with His Father. In the early mornings or late into the night, Jesus would be found with His Father. Jesus knows the Father. Jesus loves the Father. How wonderful must the Father be to captivate and satisfy the longing of the Son's heart. Once when Jesus was ministering to thousands, He dismissed the crowds and went up on the mountain by Himself to pray. He prayed well into the night. From the fatigue of ministering all day and caring for the needs of people, Jesus found comfort and rest with His Father; His rest was not in sleep.

Though we have this picture in Matthew, we must not assume this was a rare occurrence but the chief habit of Jesus. Luke told us that Jesus would spend whole nights in prayer to His Father. Mark describes how Jesus rose early in the morning, while it was still dark, to retreat to a desert place to pray. Luke said that Jesus often withdrew to deserted places to pray (Luke 5:15–16). Why was Jesus so passionate about prayer? Prayer was simply the means to an end, the end being His Father. Prayer was the opportunity of intimacy, and Jesus often retreated for this intimacy with His Father.

Jesus wanted us to know the Father. Jesus came to bring us to the Father. It was not the goal to simply keep us from hell. God desired to bring many sons to glory! So how would the people come? What would draw them? They would be drawn by love. It must be love! We love Him because He first loved us.

Who would want to spend eternity with a God of rage? But our Heavenly Father is pleasant, and this was part of Jesus' mission—to express to the world how wonderful the Father is. John 14:31 says, "... so that the world may know that I love the Father, I do exactly as the Father commanded me."

THE FATHER WANTS YOU TO BELONG TO HIM

We have to go through the Son if we want to get to the Father. There is no other way. The only way to know the Father is for the Son to reveal Him. We cannot love the Father and not love the Son. Jesus is the way, the truth, and the life. No one comes to the Father except through Him (John 14:6). Jesus said that no one knows the Son but the Father. Furthermore, no man knows the Father except the Son and those to whomsoever the Son will reveal Him (Matthew 11:25–27).

Our world is suffering an identity crisis. People do not know who or what they are. The fact is we have strayed away from our Father. God called Adam his son, but Adam rebelled, and his children were born alienated from the Father.

Men are born slaves. They have lost their identity. They spend their life under a cruel and evil tyrant, but God wants to adopt them, redeem them, and rescue them. Without belonging to the Heavenly Father we are people without a home. We are without a father. We have no identity. We have no one to love us. We feel abandoned and unwanted. We have no place we can call home, a place where we are welcomed. We are living under the curse of an unblessed life. We crave acceptance but instead only experience one betrayal after another.

The good news is that there is a Heavenly Father who wants to be your source, your guardian, your headship, your provider, your protector, your leader, your teacher, your helper, your encourager, and your friend. He left the door open for you. His Spirit cries for you to come! You can be redeemed!

This Father comforts His people and has compassion for His afflicted ones. Even in situations when it seems that the Father is distant and we may say, "The Lord has forsaken me; my Lord has forgotten me," He cries back, assuring us of His steadfast love. God declares, can a woman forget her baby nursing on her breast? Can a mother not have compassion for the child she bore? Yes! She might. "Yet," says the Lord, "even these may forget, yet I will not forget you. Behold, I

have engraved you on the palms of my hands ... [you] are
continually before Me" (Isaiah 49:15–16 ESV).

God will not forget us. God will not forsake us. Mothers
will, but God will not! When the Lord asks about the mothers
who could forget their nursing babies, He declares that we
cannot compare Him to the most profound bond upon
earth—the mother and her child.

We cannot compare the Heavenly Father with our earthly
father. We must see how the Son (Jesus) so adored His Father,
and then know that He is a good Father.

WHO ARE YOU?

When we are adopted into this family, we receive a new
identity. In this family, we are unconditionally loved! In
Psalms 139, David said the Lord was familiar and intimate
with every detail of his life, and God still loved him. David
could not think of any situation that would have caused God
to forsake him.

The Bible teaches that God formed and fashioned us. We
are not an accident. We are fearfully and wonderfully made.
God knew us before we were even born. He has planned our
lives, every detail. We are precious in His sight. The good
thoughts that God thinks toward us are too many to count.
They are more than the sand on the shores of the earth.

When David began Psalms 139, he acknowledged how
thoroughly God knew him: his sin, thoughts, and motives.
Nothing was hidden from God. Knowing God had such
wonderful thoughts about him, that He had redeemed his
heart, and had wonderfully created him, David, therefore,
throws himself upon God for examination and help. "You
search me and lead me!"

We must experience the love of God like this. We are desperate for this confidence in God's love for us. God's love is the platform of all hope and faith! The love of God is fundamental in keeping us, delivering us, and carrying us through. The love of God dispels our fears, assures us of an unfailing commitment, and secures everlasting victory. That is why I get up in the morning. I want to be with my Father. I want to spend the day with Him.

THE SHAME OF THOSE WHO DO NOT LOVE THE FATHER

My dad worked so hard. He was smart and sacrificed so much to give me all he could. I remember waiting for him to come home. I never sat there and raised my hand to wave or just say hello. I ran to him. I greeted him. Till the day he died, I kissed him. I was not an orphan. I had a father. I had a home. My father gave me foundation and purpose. I never lived wondering where I belonged, who I belonged to, or who I was. I had a place. I was free. I belonged. I was my father's son. I had a key to the house. I had access to my father that only a son could enjoy. He was mine.

Today, I watch people come into the church. It is easy to see those who enter into praise as those who belong in the family. When my dad came home, my friends would greet him. Sometimes they would even stand in respect to greet him, but they didn't have the intimacy and entry into his life that I had. We see the same in God's house. For so many who go to church, He is God, but not Father. Many respect Him. Many lift their hands to wave hello. Sometimes they may even rise in respect to honor Him, but they do not know Him as Father.

They are not comfortable in the Father's house. They have no intimacy with Him.

One can spot the children. They sing, they dance, they shout, and they rejoice. They run to the Father in the altars and kiss Him. They know who they are. They know that God loves them, and they love God. They are home.

I never grew too old to love my dad. I never took him for granted. He was my friend. He was the best man in my wedding. Why? Because he was the best man! Until I left the house, I would run to greet my father. I hug and greet people today because of my father. I love to show affection for people; my father gave me that. Like those who visit the altar, many grow out of it. They don't live at the altar. They get too old to run to the Father.

HOW LONG WILL YOU BREAK THE FATHER'S HEART?

It breaks a father's heart to have children willfully distant. A father's heart wants to be intimate. A father's heart wants to protect and provide. A father's heart seeks to nurture his children. How sad it is to have children so self-absorbed that they would spurn the father's heart. How wicked is the hardened heart that rejects the father's desires for love and belonging? It must break a father's heart. No father should experience the pain of having sons or daughters that he cannot bless.

My daughter Jordan loves me, and I love her. I give her identity and belonging. Therefore, I bless her. How ridiculous would it be if Jordan jumped up in the morning only to say hello and run out of the house being consumed with fear wondering, "What will I wear? Where will I sleep? What will

I eat?" It would break my heart to find her sleeping in my driveway because she did not know me well enough to know I had a bed prepared for her, I had a meal fixed for her, and I had rest and peace to give her. Instead, she slept out in the night, fighting June bugs, mosquitoes, and ants.

It is the Father's love that gives us freedom. It is the Father's love that gives us faith to believe that He is good and He accepts us. I am to keep myself in His love. By His love, I am delivered from fear. By His love, I am more than a conqueror. Because the Lord loved Israel, He delivered them. Because the Lord loved me, He delivered me.

If we do not know God loves us, how can you believe He will help us? Because God loves me, He is in my midst—Mighty! Because God loves me, He will save me. Because God loves me, He will rejoice over me with joy and singing. Because God loves me, I shall not be ashamed. Without love we cannot be rewarded. We cannot have hope. We cannot believe. We cannot succeed. We cannot be saved!

Without love, a girl will lay down her life to any lesser love that any man would offer. Without love, a son will bow to drugs, crime, and rebellion in a feverish attempt to be recognized. Take two small children. Show more love to one over the other and watch how that neglected child behaves. His actions will reflect the results of this lack of love. We all have an insatiable need to be loved by the Heavenly Father. He sent His only begotten Son into the world to prove He loves us.

If we are looking for a home, weary of wandering, discouraged by not having a place to belong, then the Son is waiting to bring us to the Father. Jesus will clothe us with the family robe. He will give us the family ring. We will possess the family name. All that He has can be ours. But best of all, we will have unending access to the Father. Why? Because He will be ours—our Father!

We will not be servants but adopted, His very own children. We will have His love. To have His love is to have assurance, peace, and rest. To have His love is to have power, protection, and confidence. To have His love is to have His heart. We will be more than conquerors through Him who loves us. Nothing will be able to separate us from His love, which is in Jesus Christ.

CHAPTER NOTES:

CHAPTER 5

David's Amen

In the Psalms, the singer repeatedly prepares his heart for the Lord. For example, the Psalmist prays for God to enlarge his heart, strengthen his heart, create within him a clean heart, fix his heart, and break his heart. We should do likewise. We should be in the altars before, during, and after the service to prepare our hearts to seek God. God is more interested in speaking to our hearts than our heads.

It is great negligence to simply show up for church, find a seat, listen to a preacher preach the Word of God, and have an unprepared heart. God requires much from a people with such easy and constant access to the blessing of preaching; we must prepare our hearts for this great privilege. All of us are aware of the many distractions constantly bombarding us; how easily we lose concentration. King David even wept over his divided heart, asking God to remove the many things that were pulling it in many directions.

Many people with unprepared hearts agree with God's message to their own demise. They do not understand the significance of the holy meeting between themselves and the Lord. There is an interesting moment when David said, "Amen" to a prophet's message; however, the consequence was not good for David.

In 2 Samuel, chapter 12, the prophet Nathan tells King David this story:

> There were two men in one city; the one rich and the other poor. The rich man had exceedingly many flocks and herds: but the poor man had nothing save one little ewe lamb, which he had bought and nourished up: and it grew up together with him and with his children. It did eat of his own meat, and drank of his own cup, and lay in his bosom, and was unto him as a daughter. And there came a traveler unto the rich man, and he spared to take of his own flock and of his own herd, to dress for the wayfaring man that was come unto him; but took the poor man's lamb and dressed it for the man that was come to him. David's anger was greatly kindled against the man; and he said to Nathan, "As the Lord liveth, the man who has done this thing shall surely die: And he shall restore the lamb fourfold because he did this thing and had no pity."
>
> And Nathan said to David, "Thou art the man!"

How typical is the scene? God speaks, and we heartily say "Amen" to the message of God. However, as David, we fail to see that the Word was spoken to us. I can see David agreeing with Nathan, nodding his head in agreement. Perhaps he is shouting him down, "You preach it, brother! Amen. Yes, that is the truth. Boy, I wish so and so were here to hear this."

Then, as all good preachers and prophets do, Nathan lodges the arrow of God's Word into David. Don't think of others, David. Quit dodging the truth. How long will you take God's Word as common and for others only? David, you are the man!

Nathan brought it home. As God's messenger, he doesn't throw a blanket sermon, hoping it applies to someone. The preacher knows his God, and God knows his people. When God has something to say, He does not hope it is applicable; He knows it is. God speaks on purpose. God sends His Word to accomplish His great mission. When God speaks, He has something to say—He is saying it to us!

The listener is responsible for hearing when the messenger speaks God's Word. Nevertheless, we are often like David; we amen the sermon, encourage the message, and then want to be done with the whole thing. It is the habit of shuffling in, taking our place, and casually walking out instead of praying and worshiping.

The altar is not for the lost but for those who come to thank God for His Word and desire to hide His Word in their hearts! To fail here is to fail in our responsibility as hearers. Life and death have been set before us every time the message is given. *At that point, what we do is crucial!* The problem is not merely with those who might scorn or reject the Word as nonsense. The problem is with those who love and believe it but do nothing with it. Jesus said the Word falls on all types of soil (*hearts*); some stony, some rocky, some hardened, and others prepared. If we do not have a prepared heart, the enemy will steal what God is trying to give us, or the cares of this world will choke the life out of the promises of God.

The Holy Ghost warns that all that is needed to choose death is to **NEGLECT the Word of God**! "… we must pay much closer attention to what we have heard, lest we drift away from it…. How shall we escape if we neglect?"(Hebrews 2:3 ESV). Neglect—that's a danger to believers.

Believers are not faced with the danger of disagreeing with the Word, counting God's Word as trite, or even ignoring the Word; the threat is neglect. Neglect occurs when we agree with the Word but fail to apply the Word due to carelessness. We agree with it but forget it. We love it but don't live it. The Bible warns us that we will drift away. Drifting is not a conscious effort but a slow and unnoticed wandering.

You might be asking, "So what do I do? I cannot possibly remember everything the preacher said." The answer is pretty simple, and I would like to help you by providing a contrast of examples. Consider Pharoah. Exodus 7:22 says, "Pharaoh's heart was hardened, neither did he hearken unto them as the Lord had said and Pharaoh turned and went into his house, neither did he set his heart to this also."

There are several things Pharoah did to neglect God's Word. First, he hardened his heart. To harden means to restrain or to conquer. Pharoah fought off God's Word. He refused to let it affect his heart. He battled God's attempt to reach his heart. God was not allowed to affect his life. Secondly, he did not heed the Word of the Lord. To heed means to listen with the intent to obey. When we listen to God's messengers, do we listen with the intent to obey? Third, the Word did not move his heart. To be moved is to regard and consider. He never thought twice about it.

Again, what about us? Do we ponder the words of God? Do we remember and meditate upon them? Or are we like others who could not tell what the sermon was a week ago because they fought off God's Word; by neglect they did not let the Word influence their heart? Friends, that is the purpose of the altar. The end of the service is the most critical time, for it is there at the altar we choose life. The altar is where we say to God, "Thank You for sending us Your Word. Help us to remember it and allow it to have its full effect on our lives!"

My other example is of one who cherished God's Word and found life. Her name is Mary. In Luke 2:17–19, we are told, "Now when they had seen Him, they made widely known the saying which was told them concerning this child. And all those who heard it marveled at those things which were told them by the shepherds. But Mary kept all these things and pondered them in her heart."

Many marveled at the Word. That is precisely what occurs today. As David, we marvel at the truth of the Word. We find it exciting and compelling. It comes, and we are genuinely moved and love it. However, this response is set in opposition to the correct response that Mary gave. Hearing the Word, she first kept all these things in her heart. This means to preserve them from perishing. Do we do this? Do we write and take notes, recording what God has said? Secondly, she pondered them in her heart. Other passages tell us that she hid them in her heart. Not her mind, but her heart. To ponder means to consider and fight to understand.

In our examples, there is one common occurrence—the heart! It is a matter of the heart. "You have said, 'Seek my face,' my **heart** says to you, 'Your face, Lord, do I seek'" (Psalms 27:8 ESV) God tells us this in Proverbs 4:4, "He also taught me, and said to me: 'Let your **heart** retain my words; Keep my commands, and live.'" The heart is the seat of our will and passions. God wants us to feel His Word. His Word is to be grafted into our will, providing convictions that will make us godly!

The parable of the Sower talks about good soil and bad soil to make a point. The Word of God falls upon both; however, it will only take root and bring forth life in good soil. The condition of your heart (whether it is good soil or bad) is in your hands. God grants you the liberty to be a *Pharoah* or a *Mary*. It is your choice!

WHEN OUR HEARTS AGREE WITH GOD

Confession is the key to walking in the light. Peter did not confess Jesus (which means to agree with) and walked in a night of great darkness, being sifted by Satan! When the Holy Spirit reaches us with His Word, the hearers must respond for the complete planting of that message into their hearts. So much is lost by silence and lack of confession. Believers should respond to the sermon! Words of confession (agreement) should echo around the room: "Amen! That's right! God is speaking to me!" There needs to be confession.

We must agree with the Lord and the truth He declares at the altar, and every time a truth knocks on our hearts. Agreement is a sure way of opening the heart as Mary did; this allows entrance for the Word. Sadly, our response to the Word of God has been conditioned by a very stale western culture.

This tradition is in direct contradiction to the demands of God. Even our altar services have become tradition used by those who are being saved or rededicating their life to God. However, in the Bible the altar was intended for believers who desired to worship, celebrate, and praise God. This very truth will be ignored by countless believers who will refuse to bow to God week after week; it is just not their custom to do so though it is the culture of heaven.

Confession overcomes the spirit of carnality and a lack of expectancy within the service. When confession is made, agreement occurs; and the presence of Jesus is more manifest than before. Thus, a few members confessing agreement with the sermon can prevail over a complacent congregation and therefore receive the manifest Spirit of Christ, providing a blessing for the whole assembly. The lazy can still have the experience of His presence because the hungry confess, and they receive what they believe God for.

THE ALTAR AND A PREPARED HEART

When we speak of the altar, it is evident that our altar is always and forever the sacrifice of Jesus on the cross. Our reference to the Word *altar* represents a place and time where believers do business with God: cry, pray, celebrate, and praise. We believe God is there, and our heart desires Him. We believe that He is and we must seek Him. It can be anywhere in the room. However, Hebrews 13 tells us that we should go out to Him "... By Him therefore let us offer the sacrifice of praise to God continually, that is, the fruit of our lips giving thanks to His name" (Hebrews 13:13, 14).

Peter called us priests of the Lord. We are privileged to lead the worship of God. Leadership is never done in private or from the back. It is always upfront and visible. "Ye also, as lively stones, are built up a spiritual house, an holy priesthood, to offer up spiritual sacrifices, acceptable to God by Jesus Christ…. Ye are a chosen generation, a royal priesthood, an holy nation, a peculiar people; that ye should shew forth the praises of Him who hath called you out of darkness into His marvelous light" (1 Peter 2:5, 9).

We are supposed to show the praises of God. People are supposed to see us praising God, honoring God, and celebrating God. The place where we gather together with the particular focus of honoring and calling upon the name of the Lord is what we call the altar. Call it what we will. Call it the gathering, the choir of praise, but for God's sake, let the priests of the Lord show forth His praise!

The altar is where the heart can express its pursuit of God. The place where we take our shoes off. We are on holy ground. The question is not, "Why do we have to go?" but "Why would we not want to go?"

Many churches are dying from the unbelief that says, "Why do I have to go to the altar?" As Naaman, they even feel contempt to suggest that I must bathe in Jordan to be healed. The blind man could have suggested, "Why do I have to go to the pool of Siloam to wash?" Daniel could have reasoned; "I can pray anywhere. Why must I open my window and pray where my enemies can see? I can pray secretly; after all, God is looking at my heart." Mary had to leave her house and go outside to meet Jesus. Jesus is the God; we must go to Him!

Moreover, hear the testimony of many we admire telling us repeatedly, "There is just something unique about being at the altar with so many people crying out to God. There is something different."

CHURCHES WITH NO ALTAR

Please imagine the church having no altar. Actually, we don't have to imagine. Most churches do not have an altar. So consider the churches where there is no altar. No life. No power. No presence. No miracles. No joy. No participation. Is that the kind of church we want to have? Nobody is taking the lead up front and crying out to God. Nobody responds in joyful faith. Nobody is getting help from the body. Would we like for our church to be like that? Would God want our church like that?

Where the Spirit is not allowed to move, there is no altar. Where the Spirit is moving, there is an altar. Those of us not in an altar, may I ask, "Where are your children? Are they in church with you? Are they walking with God?" What is the value of your faith if those closest to you don't want to follow? God always demanded a response to His Word and His presence. Beloved, let our hearts worship God. Let our hearts draw near to God. Let our hearts rejoice. Let our hearts be happy in Jesus, and let others see; this is our priestly privilege!

CHAPTER NOTES:

CHAPTER 6

A Man to Be Envied

T wo thousand years of church history has produced a full spectrum of personalities and particular religious camps. Today, there is an array of doctrinal beliefs from holiness to "greasy grace" and from "name it and claim it" prosperity to poverty. These beliefs are mixed with dangerous doctrines of devils, as the Bible prophesied.

It is not difficult to discern the camp to which a believer belongs. The personality and character of a person, right down to how they dress, bears the image of their pet doctrine.

There is a hunger within all of God's people for the things of God. Every Christian camp would confess that they desire God and wish to honor Him. Every camp of religious persuasion would seek a solid and intimate prayer life. Indeed, all who pursue God, hunger and yearn for His abiding presence. However, which method is correct? What is true spirituality? What characterizes the man who longs for

God? What is he like? Is he jovial or stern? Is he happy or sad? Is he inviting or intimidating?

Let's take a look at Psalm 84 and find the portrait of the man who walks in holiness before God. Notice the spiritual longing. This is not the devotion of some flaky amateur or someone seeking a feel-good-make-me-happy contemporary church service. There is a real need in this man. He has passion. Notice the yearning, the fainting, the crying out, the awesome prayer life: My soul longs and faints for the courts of the Lord. My heart and flesh cry out for God (Psalms 84).

A BLESSED MAN IS A HAPPY MAN

The Bible describes the man who is holy and close to God as **BLESSED!** To be blessed means to be happy and have a life envied by others. He is not austere—which is to be stern, strict, and grim in one's appearance. The austere personality who claims to be spiritual is deceived. Their serious mindset may seem authentic, but their holiness of life is unreal. The Bible says that *joy and cheerfulness* characterize those who walk with God! Again, notice the man in Psalms 84.

- Blessed are they that dwell in your house. They are not depressed and sad; they are full of praise.

- Blessed is the man who has God for his strength.

- Blessed is the man whose heart is filled with the ways of God.

- Blessed is the man who has God to trust.

WHY ARE THEY TO BE ENVIED?

Psalms 84 continues to show us this blessed life and the reasons the blessed man is to be envied—why he is happy:

- His life makes the barren places fruitful.
- He goes from strength to strength.
- He has access to God.
- God hears his prayers.
- God is his shield.
- God gives him grace and glory.
- God gives him every good thing.

If people who desire God don't admire and envy us, then something is wrong with our spirituality. People who want to be like Jesus but don't want to be like us should reveal that something is wrong with us! If godly people can't fellowship with us, then we are unlike Christ and our spirituality is a farce! John said, "... that which we have seen and heard declare we unto you, that you also may have fellowship with us; and truly our fellowship is with the Father and with His Son Jesus Christ. And these things we write to you that your joy may be full!" (1 John 1:3)

A preacher once said that many Christians are not happy because they are not holy; they are not holy because they are not filled, and they are not filled because they are not separate. The Holy Spirit will not fill what He cannot separate. Whom He cannot fill He will not make holy, and whom He can't make holy will not be happy.

The Bible says that the man who walks with God passes through the valley of Baca and makes it a well (Psalms 84). The valley of Baca is the valley of tears. It denotes the image of weeping. Even here, in a season where many suffer pain, heartache, and despair, those who walk with God are refreshing. Through their familiarity with God, they transform the barren and hopeless places of life into a spring of joy and expectation! These blessed souls are sought out when calamity strikes. In tragedy, we don't want the depressed and austere. We don't want the soulish and emotional. We want those who know God and who can be used by God to transform night into day and mourning into dancing!

WHY ARE THEY SO HAPPY?

Those who walk with God are happy. They are happy because God is their strength! Who can overcome a person if God is their strength? What force or invading horde can threaten their safety when they dwell in the arms of the Mighty God? What scenario could possibly depress them if it is God who works all things together for their good? Who can stand against them if God is for them?

These people are happy because God is their sun and shield! He is a sun for the happy days and a shield for the dangerous days. Because He is a defense around His people, no weapon formed against them can prosper! Those who walk with God are happy because they have someone to trust. "For a day in thy courts is better than a thousand. I had rather be a doorkeeper in the house of my God, than to dwell in the tents of wickedness. For the Lord God is a sun and shield: the Lord will give grace and glory. No good thing will He withhold from them that walk uprightly" (Psalms 84:10–12).

They are happy because God is the joy of their life! A day in God's courts is better than a thousand elsewhere. To open doors for God brings more honor than being a king over the wicked.

I can testify of the joy that Jesus is to me. All my joy is in Him. He is the source of all my expectations, and He delights in me. I am happier now when I am unhappy than I was before when I was happy. Some Christians must search for things to cheer them up because they are not joyful. They are not joyful because they have not been with God!

A man must know the Lord by the life of real faith, or he cannot rejoice in the Lord's worship, be at home in the Lord's house, take delight in the Lord's Son, or commit himself to the Lord's ways!

What a relief it is to have someone on your side. What comfort to have a companion. And when that companion is the Lord God Almighty, then how exceedingly abundant is the comfort and support. Think of it; I have somebody to trust. What is my fear? I can trust Him! What is my worry? I can trust Him! What is my problem? I can trust Him!

Lord, You are my Light and my Savior, so why should I be afraid of anyone? The Lord is where my life is safe, so I will be afraid of no one! Evil people might attack me. They might try to destroy my body. Yes, my enemies might attack and try to destroy me, but they will stumble and fall. Even if an army surrounds me, I will not be afraid. Even if people attack me in war, I will trust in the Lord. I ask only one thing from the Lord. This is what I want most: Let me live in the Lord's house all my life, enjoying the Lord's beauty and spending time in his palace. He will protect me when I am in danger. He will hide me in His tent. He will take me up to His place of safety. (Psalms 27:1–5 ERV)

It is good for the ungodly when they see Christians glad; they long to be believers themselves. It is suitable for our fellow Christians to see happy Christians, for it comforts them and tends to cheer them. It is an unfortunate thing for the Christian to become depressed. If there is any man in the world who has a right to be happy, it is the man whose sins are forgiven—the man who lives in the secret place with God.

CHAPTER NOTES:

CHAPTER 7

The Heart Of Worship

How does God measure a man? Does He take a poll for the most popular candidate? File through the list of leading theologians of the day? Search the pool of intelligent, influential, and prominent men? What would constitute a real man? Would God take the measurements of their shoulders or their hearts? Would God test the strength of their arms and legs or examine the strength of their spirit? Would He review the vows, promises, and dreams so many have made, or would He consider their devotion and integrity?

I think we already know what God is after in man. "Oh, that there was such an heart in them…" (Deuteronomy 5:29). God is looking at our hearts! It is the heart that reveals the kind of people we are.

God looked down upon humankind. Why? To see if any understood. God's conclusion: they are all corrupt and have done abominable iniquity; no one does good—their foolish hearts say there is no god (Psalm 53)! How tragic. How sad.

And God cried. He cried so the hearts of His creation would hear: "… [you] have removed [your] heart far from Me" (Isaiah 29:13). It was not that our hearts got distracted or cold; we removed our hearts from God. All the Lord wanted was for us to love Him wholeheartedly; but we did not. (Deuteronomy 6:5).

Is there hope? Can anything be different? Can we love God with our hearts? Because of grace, the answer is, "YES!" God will saturate our hearts with His love if we allow it (Romans 5:5). There have been men and women who experienced this grace. The Bible calls them worshipers. God is still looking for these worshipers today.

What was it about David that attracted God? It had to be the faith in David's heart. With his whole heart, David praised God. We will not see many men in our churches praising God this way. Maybe with a half-heart some will praise God, but what a rare sight to see a man praising God wholeheartedly. David's response to God was from the heart. When God told David to seek His face, David responded in his heart. David's heart said, "Thy face, Lord, will I seek" (Psalms 27:8). David's heart was all in. "The Lord is my strength and my shield; my heart trusted in Him … my heart greatly rejoiceth; and with my song will I praise Him" (Psalms 28:7).

There was the passion of worship in David. David loved the Lord. With his whole heart, David sought the Lord. He took God's Word and hid it in his heart. God was real to David. God was worth pursuing and even better at catching. Every day was a brand-new pursuit of God: "O God, thou art my God; early will I seek thee: my soul thirsteth for thee, my flesh longeth for thee in a dry and thirsty land, where no water is" (Psalms 63:1).

You may assume that David's words are just poetry. This assumption reveals our world's problem. God is not real to people. Worship is not authentic. People who claim to love God have removed their hearts far from Him. But not David; David will seek God early. David will go to church looking for the power and glory of God. When others are content with their dry and barren hearts, David will run hard after God, "As the hart panteth after the water brooks, so panteth my soul after thee, O God. My soul thirsteth for God, for the living God: when shall I come and appear before God?" (Psalms 42:1–2).

A HEART FOR WORSHIP

David! There is a man for you—a man after God's own heart. He was a man doing what he was created to do, and God enjoyed his love and worship. Today, so many believers want to be used and do something for God. Why is there no heart of worship in us? Many think they would be happy and satisfied if they could have some great ministry. No! Satisfaction is intimacy with God, not working for God. Period. Nothing else. Everything else is a by-product of our worship. Likewise, every evil thing is a by-product of our lack of worship.

"If others could see me… Suppose people could see my gift. If God touched and made me great, I would have value." This is the frequent cry of so many I encounter around the world. Beloved, wake up! Quit with this charade. Beloved, in His presence is the fullness of joy. Instead of turning our heart back to God, we continue to live hoping for someone to see and appreciate us, when all along God is inviting us to draw near. He also says to us, "Seek my face." But what will our hearts say?

All David wanted was God. However, look at the life of this man who caught hold of God. In every area of his life, he is consequential, animating, and provocative! Even when it came to sin and disgrace, even in this, David did it with all his might. David's life is full. Whether displaying his brilliance on the battlefield, his failure as a father, his timeless worship and songs, or his unrivaled empire as king—his life is full!

When did it start for David? It started with his devotion, probably when he was about eight years old. He lay under the stars and beheld God's wonders as his sheep sighed in the distance. David was alive before God, and the longing of God's heart changed his life! David knew that God wanted a relationship with him. David cried, "When I consider the Heavens the work of your fingers, the moon and the stars, which you have ordained, what is man that You are mindful of him, and the son of man that You visit him?" This knowledge about God forever changed David and thus compelled his heart upon its worthy pursuit—fellowship with the Living God. A living man must have a Living God. God must be experienced; words and doctrines will not be sufficient.

If David is a man after God's own heart, it must have crushed him to hear the horrifying cry of God as He looked upon His creation, seeking a worshiper. How can people know God exists yet not pursue Him? It is not the atheist committing the abomination before God; it is the one who knows God exists but does not seek Him wholeheartedly. It's the one who says in his heart, not with his mouth, that there is no God. In other words, it is the one who believes in God but lives as though He does not exist. Could there be any greater offense against Heaven's Most Righteous King?

David quickly realized the question was not "where is God?" Or "why doesn't He speak to me and help me?" It is not the questions *men* ask. No. The question is the one *God* asks, and God's question has not changed. As in the Garden of Eden, the question was and always had been, "Adam, where are you? David, where are you?" God is searching. We were not looking for Him, but He does look for us! Indeed, this became the question of David. After all, a man after God's heart can only have one question anyway—"God, what does Your heart want?" David found out! God shared with David that no one was seeking Him!

Jesus made it undeniably clear when He said that the Father seeks those who are true worshipers. True worshipers are not people who confess there is a God but those whose whole lives reflect that belief. Those who pursue God in Spirit and Truth shall worship the Father, for these are the ones the Father seeks! Now that doesn't exclude us. Don't get into that self-pity notion that thinks, "Because we can't sing or dance or cry about the things of God like other people seem to do, we are not included." Paul told us that without faith it is impossible to please God, for we must believe that He is and that He is a rewarder of those who diligently seek Him.

So many of us believe that He is, but we don't diligently seek Him! That is the ultimate offense! God is not what we want. We only seek Him for what He can give! We think, "If I can get close to God, I can get my healing, money, fame, prosperity, or a new job." God is so rarely wanted for Himself. He is pursued for *things*. People preach Him for money, and contemporary Christian entertainers want God to make them famous; churches are built for crowds, not for the fearsome presence of the Holy God.

Churches are run today by skill, not God. He is not needed! And dare we touch the "Christian home" today! One glance at the average Christian home would have to make one ask why they call themselves Christian! The teenagers are just like the world, and the parents are no better. Let's come on and ask ourselves if we live like there is an awesome, loving, faithful God! If we do, why are we so often worried? Why are we stressed out? Why do we seek so much of the world? Why are we raising our kids, emphasizing the devil's world rather than God's world? How can we get them to school five days a week, but can't get them to Sunday school one day a week? Why don't we have more time for God during the day? Why don't we pray more? Why isn't there more passion for God? Why do our faces say that God has forsaken us? Why don't we wake up with Him on our minds? Why can't we lie awake at night and think about God? Oh, I know we believe in God ... and God knows we believe in Him ... He wants to know how long we will continue making excuses for neglecting Him and breaking His heart.

THE REWARD

How does one live who believes with all his heart that God is a rewarder of those who diligently seek Him? In the sixty-third Psalm, the man after God's heart responded to the cry of the searching God. "Oh God, You are my God; early will I seek You; My soul thirsts for You; My flesh longs for You." When I come to church, I come for Him. I have looked for him in the sanctuary to see His power and glory. I don't know why some people come. Perhaps they come to show their new wardrobe. Or maybe it is a time to see friends and make plans for the week. Perhaps it is because they are in a bind and need the assistance of God: sin may be weighing heavily upon them, they may be wrestling with their health, or their home may be in derision. But David said, "I come for You."

Certainly, it is not wrong to bring all our needs to the altar and cast all our cares upon the Lord, and it is wonderful to enjoy the body of Christ and look forward to seeing our friends and loved ones in church. However, the passion is for God. We want to see Him! We want to behold His power. We want to worship in fear and awe before Him. More than anything else, and stronger than any other motive, is our desire to "faith" our way into His presence to worship Him.

Singing is not worship. Lifting hands, though a form of praise, is not worship. Today, we think praise and worship is the music and singing part of the service. Worship, however, is to see and tremble before God. David was determined to have this experience. David's heart said, "I will not be bored … I will not be distracted … I do not need to be entertained … I will not sleep … I will look for You in the sanctuary!"

Expectation has always been present in the church in the times of her greatest power. When the church believed, she expected, and her Lord never disappointed her. Every great movement of God in history, every unusual advance in the church, and every revival has been preceded by keen anticipation. Expectations accompanied the operations of the Spirit always. His bestowals hardly surprised His people because they were gazing expectantly toward the risen Lord and looking confidently for His Word to be fulfilled. His blessings accorded with their expectations. One characteristic that marks the average church today is a lack of anticipation. When they meet, Christians do not expect anything unusual to happen; consequently, only the usual happens, and that is as predictable as the sun's setting.

THE OVERWHELMING GOD

If we have ever been with God, then He overwhelms us. His loving kindness is better than life. Our hearts lose composure; our lips break forth with praise. We love to talk about Him and extol Him. This is not a Sunday talk followed by a Monday talk; but while we live, we bless the Lord. We lift our hands unto His name. We want everyone to know how much we love God—how wonderful He is, and how delighted we are to be in love with Him!

When our hearts are aware of God, our whole transports are moved. Our heart cannot compose the joy. We lay on the bed and just think about Him. Most nights, we cannot sleep as our heart races with the pleasure of seeing Him face to face. Just thinking about Jesus causes our soul to rapture and stirs us from my slumber.

So many lie awake in fear and look out for enemies, but we watch for God. "Are You summoning me into Your presence? Are You longing to be with me tonight? Dare I let sleep come between us? If you look to see if men are seeking You, You will indeed find one, for I lie awake on my bed and speak of You and fill my heart and mind with thoughts of You. My soul follows hard after You. You can't get rid of me! I would rather die than not have You!"

What are we willing to do to keep your jobs? How hard do we fight for our rights and respect? If only some of us would fight half as hard for the knowledge of God as we do for ourselves, what then?

We can't love a theological Jesus with passion. "Things" can't satisfy a living soul. If "things" are satisfying, it's because the soul is sick and dying! Our souls thirst for what: an abstraction, a possession, riches, or something else? No! Our souls thirst for the Living God! Life thirsts for life as the spirit craves spirit. David wanted someone to love and touch. David didn't seek his satisfaction in many lives but one LIFE—God!

If a man is to be blessed, he must have one source to which he can go. Christians have never been busier: meetings, appointments, functions, rehearsals, clubs, banquets, studies, committees, and retreats. Christians have a very dynamic relationship in the things of God, but not a fresh day-by-day relationship with God. Martin Luther said it is much easier to do a thousand masses daily than to say one true prayer. Another leader from the past said, "Much of our religious activity today is nothing more than a cheap anesthetic to deaden the pain of an empty life!"

I have been so thankful to God for calling our church into a prayer revival. In recent years, the Lord called us as a church to seek Him diligently. Since this call and our step of obedience, we have seen the manifest presence of God in our services and preaching. Scores of people have testified to me of the dramatic changes in their spiritual lives and relationships with God. They have fallen in love with God Himself. They have come to love the prayer meeting for its apprehending of God over any other service we have! I think this is a beautiful testimony of the beauty and delight of our God.

To become spiritual, we do not need to become active. Action is the result of spirituality. Our life is in Him, not in what we do for Him. This is why so many suffer burnout. They labor to become somebody or to attain something and only end up complicating their life. We are made in the image of God to communicate with a world we cannot see. Our comrades are angels, archangels, and seraphim, yet we are settling down here with the temporal.

The human's reproach is the tyranny of things: material things, temporal things, things that are and then cease to be. We are made for walking with God, yet we choose to walk with devils. We are made to correspond with the Almighty, yet we choose to spend our time in front of a television. We are fashioned for eternity and shall continue when this world, and all in it, has long been burned up, and yet we continue to lay up our treasure here.

Of all God's creatures, are any more pathetic? Man is insensible and blind and deaf in his eagerness to forget that there is a God! Man is a fool to embrace this strange belief that materialism and humanism constitute the "good life." Tozer said, "I would rather be a Muslim or a Hindu or a primitive tribesman living in a cootie-infested hut in Africa, kneeling before bones and feathers and mumbling some kind of home-made prayer, than to come into judgment as a self-sufficient American businessman who ruled God out of his life and out of his business and out of his home."

Early in his life, we see a determination in David that forever sustained him. Such determination was witnessed during his highly publicized bout with Goliath; he would rather die fighting for God than live betraying Him. David stood alone in his convictions of God's power and faithfulness. He was willing to put himself through overwhelming odds so that others may know there is a God in Israel. We must believe that we are those agents. This is faith in God—that He will use us! Not to know He *can*, but that He *will*!

A man cannot seek God until God has sought the man. Once prompted, there is no limit to where a man can go. Let's consider ourselves prompted. David went to total absorption with the Almighty. And what is His most incredible legacy? Undoubtedly, it would have to be His son Jesus the Christ!

CHAPTER NOTES:

CHAPTER 8

He Is With Us

And to us who have fled for refuge to lay hold upon the hope that is set before us in the gospel, how unutterably sweet is the knowledge that our Heavenly Father knows us completely. No tale bearer can inform on us, no enemy can make an accusation stick; no forgotten skeleton can come tumbling out of some hidden closet to abash us and expose our past; no unsuspected weakness in our characters can come to light to turn God away from us, since He knew us utterly before we knew Him and called us to Himself in the full knowledge of everything that was against us. For the mountains shall depart, and the hills be removed; but my kindness shall not depart from thee, neither shall the covenant of my peace be removed, saith the Lord that hath mercy on thee.

Our Father in heaven knows our frame and remembers that we are dust. He knew our inborn treachery, and for His own sake, engaged to save us.(Isaiah 48:8-11) His only Begotten Son, when He walked among us, felt our pains in their naked intensity of anguish. His knowledge of our afflictions and adversities is more than theoretic; it is personal, warm, and compassionate. Whatever may befall us, God knows and cares as no one else can (A.W. Tozer, The Knowledge of The Holy).

God's rescue mission was not simply pity for doomed creatures made in His image. He was not content to simply pull them out of danger; He would restore and adopt them as His children. He desired to bring them into a place of great favor and intimacy. The question is not how sinners can have fellowship with God, but how can God, Who is holy, have a relationship with sinners?

God is not some divine lifeguard, but a redeemer willing to save us from drowning in our sins. He is not a rescue worker who wants to deliver us from struggling in the cesspool of life. He is not even a compassionate judge who longs for a way to excuse our crimes. Instead, He is consumed with us. He longs for a relationship with us. He wants to be with us.

So how can God do it? How can He legally join Himself to those who are sinners? Hebrews 2 reveals that Jesus became a man to suffer death so that by the grace of God He could taste death for every man. Every man! Not just good men (for no man is good). Not just righteous men (for no man is righteous). By this grace of sacrifice, Jesus could bring us to glory. Not only could Jesus save us from hell, but He could also perfect us and make us one with Himself. He could call us brothers by means of imputed righteousness. This means that those who trust Jesus to sanctify them are as holy and perfect as Jesus, who sanctifies!

Jesus came and by death destroyed death and the devil. Through the cross, Jesus wrecked the powers of Satan and delivered men from the bondage and fear of death. He now serves as our High Priest with great mercy and reconciles us to the Father.

Now, through the atonement, God has saved us and brought us near to Himself to be with Him and He with us. He is with us! He can be anywhere, but He is with us! He is everywhere, but He is with us! He is not rooting for us; He is with us! He is not leading; He is carrying us; He is not coaching us; He is gracing us!

The Jesus in heaven acts just like the Jesus on earth. His compassion upon the outcast, the sinful, the children, the unclean, the sick, and the prostitutes is the same now as it was when He was on earth. He saved then; He saves now. He wanted the sinner then; He wants the sinner now. Jesus' desire to see Peter after his public denial is the same desire that Jesus has to see you.

There is safety in Jesus. There is tragedy outside of Jesus. Wrath, death, torment, and condemnation await all who do not trust in Jesus' sacrifice. Jesus wants us to come to Him. He wants us to come so that He can save us from His unvented wrath against sin. He died to make reconciliation for the sins of His people. If we are not "His people," then we are still in our sins and will face the judgment of God.

Not only does Jesus want to save us from this condemnation, but He also wants us to be with Him in joy and life. He wants us to experience the joy and love of His

Father. Jesus prayed in John 17:24, "Father, I will that they also, whom thou hast given me, be with me where I am; that they may behold my glory, which thou hast given me: for thou lovedst me before the foundation of the world."

The Bible declares in Hebrews 2 that we are one with Jesus and He is not ashamed to call us brothers. Considering all our failures, sins, and abuses, it is a fantastic hope to know that we can spend eternity in the love and joy of God without ever being ashamed! God knows where we have been, what we have done, and why we did it, and He wants to sanctify us wholly so we can live joyfully with Him. How marvelous.

I want to take a moment to consider how Jesus is our merciful High Priest. Hebrews 2 reveals how Jesus became a man. He was not a superman—like an angel among us. He was a man. He suffered from hunger, anguish, rejection, and so forth. He knows what shame is. He knows personally what it feels like to be abandoned, to feel embarrassed, to be misunderstood, and to be falsely accused.

A HIGH PRIEST WITH MERCY

Jesus' pity or mercy for us is not as an animal lover pitying a suffering animal. The Bible says He feels our pain. He is drawn to our suffering and engaged in delivering and healing us. He knows the torment of a trusted friend forsaking us, and He immediately goes into action to console us. When we are overwhelmed with sorrow, Jesus understands because He also was overwhelmed with grief.

The sufferings Jesus experienced were beyond personal. The chastisement of our peace was upon Him. His stripes heal us. God laid the iniquity of us all upon Him. His weakness and suffering experiences are central to His High Priestly work.

He is assigned by the Father to take care of us—not only when we are doing good, but also when we are failing, sinning, and suffering. Jesus is engaged on our behalf. Jesus is not loyal only when we are. Jesus is loyal when we are not. Jesus is not only faithful when we are faithful; Jesus is faithful when we are not.

When we have lost confidence in ourselves, when our lives are spiraling out of control, when there is no way we can pull ourselves up, here comes our High Priest with mercy. He is not confident in us to follow His instructions. He is confident in Himself to be all we need.

A HIGH PRIEST WHO CAN BE TOUCHED

When we suffer, He is touched. When we are tempted, He is touched. When we are broken, He is touched. Understand that every time we are betrayed, wounded, hurt, or persecuted, it touches Him. According to Hebrews 2, He is one with us.

Hebrews 4:15 says that we have a High Priest who is touched by the feelings of our infirmity. He is not like a doctor who just knows we are sick and knows how to heal us. The feeling of our pain touches Him. The bowels of His compassion erupt within Him. Picture a mother holding her helpless, suffering child in an emergency room, and we can begin to see the compassion that Jesus has for us. He holds us like that. That is how the mercy comes to us. We are not patients; we are His brothers; we are one with Jesus. It matters to Him.

But we say, "Then where is God when we hurt? Why does He seem to not care? Why doesn't He help us?" It is because we must access what is flowing out of His heart. He is not holding back mercy, like a dam holding back water, and we somehow feel we must find a way to break the dam. He is not withholding grace. Instead, we are not receiving the abundance of mercy extended to us. We must "come boldly unto the throne of grace" (Hebrews 4:16) to obtain mercy and find the grace in difficult times.

Not even our sin restrains the Father's grace. Even then, Jesus is touched by our infirmities, and He is drawn to us with the utmost concern and help. Jesus is not our High Priest because we do not need forgiveness. He is our High Priest because we need forgiveness. Jesus is not our High Priest because we have no sin; Jesus is our High Priest because we sin (1 John 2:1).

Jesus will transform all these painful experiences into strength. He alone can work everything together for our good. The good that Jesus is working for us is changing us so that we will be conformed to His image.

A HIGH PRIEST WHO MAKES US GREAT

When we continue to suffer or sin, Jesus does not despair. He knows He can perfect us. He knows that His blood has made atonement for us. He knows our death has been defeated. He knows because He made atonement for us; He destroyed our death. Jesus is not worried about His ability to sanctify us. He is joyfully gentle in His dealings with us. There is no cloud of judgment over us; no impending wrath is headed our way; Jesus has taken it away.

What did David mean when he said God's gentleness made him great? In Psalms 18, David said, "Thou hast also given me the shield of thy salvation: and thy right hand hath holden me up, and thy gentleness hath made me great. Thou hast enlarged my steps under me, that my feet did not slip."

David deserved judgment. David deserved the harshness of God, but instead, God was gentle. God did not beat David when he was down, but picked him up. Likewise, if we humble ourselves before God and come to the throne of grace, we will be given mercy. The gentleness of God will make us great. God's mercy toward us has nothing to do with the greatness of our sin, but with whether or not we come to Him with it. The devil would tell us to hide our sin from God. All of history tells us this is foolish. The cross tells us to bring our sins to God. All the saints tell us this is freedom.

WHAT WILL JESUS DO WITH US?

Do we struggle to believe that we will be given mercy when we fail? We can believe this for others, but not for ourselves. We knew better; we promised and vowed to God that we would be good, but we have failed. Now, how could those like us be given mercy? Is there any hope?

Is there something in the Bible that can assure us that if we come to God with our infirmities, He will be faithful to us? Yes, there is. "All that the Father giveth me shall come to me; and him that cometh to me I will in no wise cast out" (John 6:37). In no wise! He will never cast us out. In no wise! No exceptions. No three strikes and we are out. No sin too bad. No sinners too rebellious. Whoever (that is us) comes to Me (that is Jesus), I will in no wise cast out.

There is no excuse for us not to come. Those words from John 6:37 were spoken on purpose for us because Jesus knew we would find it hard to believe that God loves us. He knew we would think we are the exception; we would think we are that one person God hates; we are that sinner that is too bad to be saved. So Jesus made it plain—him (put your name in place of him) that comes to me I will in NO WISE cast out.

If we come to Jesus, we will not be cast out. If we do not come to Jesus, we will be cast out. Beloved, come! Stop listening to Satan as he tells us God does not want to be with us. The Spirit and the bride say, "Come!" Come and find grace and mercy.

CHAPTER NOTES:

CHAPTER 9

Give Me The Feet

When we bow before God, where are we? At his feet! A.W. Tozer said, "Our great weakness is that not only are we not going on to know Christ in rich intimacy of acquaintance but we're not even talking about it. We don't even hear about it. It doesn't get into our magazines. It doesn't get into our books. It doesn't get onto our radios. It's not found in our churches—this yearning, this longing to know Him in increasing measure."

When our spiritual lives become defined by the *routine* of the spiritual: the routine of Bible study, attending Sunday School, or faithfulness to the Prayer Meeting—when that becomes the focus, then we have lost the worshiping heart! If the Bible study, the Sunday School, or the Prayer Meeting are no longer a means by which we can walk in rich intimacy with God, then we have exchanged the love of God for the practice of religion.

I have often wondered if God is walking in our churches saying, "Where are you?" if the silent replies would be, "God, we are buried in Bible study. God, we are busy working in the ministry. God, we are over here, out in the streets evangelizing for you!" And God would still say, "Where are you? Where is our relationship? Where is our fellowship? This is all that I want!"

God is not looking for the active life; He is looking for the worshiping heart, "For the eyes of the LORD run to and fro throughout the whole earth, to show himself strong in the behalf of *them* whose heart *is* perfect toward him" (2 Chronicles 16:9).

From the beginning of time to now, God is searching; He is looking. He is walking through the earth looking into every one of us, into our souls! He is not looking at our lifted hands or the noises our voices make, as though He is fooled by our outward actions. God observes our hearts and is attentive to the cry of our souls. He is aware when our body language betrays our hearts. However, when our hearts can express affection for God through outward demonstrations: bowing, lifting of the hands, voices raised in singing and shouting, declarations of praise, then this is received by the Lord as worship. But make no mistake, God is looking into our hearts.

This seeking God wants to be with us! Do we get it? All that is required is that we want Him from the heart! We can bring God nothing else, just the worshiping heart; nothing else is going to impress Him, not our tithes, fasting, or religion! Our aspirations to have fellowship with God is what He most desires. The motivation of God in redemption and adoption was to be our Father, not our boss.

The great heart of our Heavenly Father is filled with love! What does He want? Jesus told us when we pray, say, "Our Father …" This is what God wants us to understand! As our Father, He wants to be strong for us because we are weak. He wants us to come to Him with the faith of a child. That is all. God is not looking for the strong. God is not counting on those who have come through seminary, confident in their doctrines, carrying their credentials, and trained to take on the world. God is not looking for a man who has memorized the scriptures and can answer every question! God wants weak people. God is looking for those who need a Father! God wants the feeble so that He may be strong for them.

Paul fainted for this God! Paul counted everything that distracted him from knowing Jesus Christ as dung. He refused to let anything interfere with this one goal. He would not let missions, preaching, or church issues interfere with knowing Christ. Paul would forgo this world, its fame, and accolades to have Jesus Christ!

GOD WANTS TO BE YOUR FATHER

Do we ever wonder why God has a bride, or why God reveals Himself as a Father? Why does God want to be the "LOVER" of my soul? Why do we sing, "Jesus, lover of my soul …"

Why does God keep all our tears in His bottle? Why does God engrave us on the palms of His hands? Why does God number our hairs? Why did God write the Song of Solomon? He did these things so that dead religious men could not define love with God. Jesus doesn't show up in our churches because He loves praise. He shows up because He loves us. Do we love the Lord?

God does not have many friends. We want the Lord when our babies are sick. We want the Lord when a loved one has been diagnosed with an incurable disease. We want the Lord when the job is on the line. We want the Lord when our finances are failing. We want the Lord at the wedding but not the reception. In other words, we like the fact that there is a God who will help us, but few are friends who seek to spend time with Him daily. Few are the lovers who lie awake at night—love-sick for God, astounded by His beauty. Few are those who consider the treasures of this world as dung compared to knowing Jesus.

GOD DOES NOT HAVE MANY FRIENDS

Many are those who want Him in their homes and like having Him near, but how many are like Mary who kiss His feet? There is a legacy with the worshiper that is not found in the preacher, the teacher, the singer, or the elder. Jesus asked Peter, "Do you love me more than these?" The same could be asked of us. Do we love Jesus, period? Not for the things He can give us or the life He can bless us with, but simply for Him. Will we bear His reproach? "Let us go forth therefore unto him without the camp, bearing his reproach. For here have we no continuing city, but we seek one to come. By him therefore let us offer the sacrifice of praise to God continually, that is, the fruit of *our* lips giving thanks to his name" (Hebrews 13:13–15).

What does it mean "to bear His reproach?" We give Jesus our hearts and our love, and He gives us His reproach. What exactly does this mean? It means that if we love the reproach of Jesus, then we will surely love the best of Jesus! This is what it means—it means that the most difficult thing about Jesus is beautiful to us.

"And he turned to the woman, and said unto Simon, Seest thou this woman? I entered into thine house, thou gavest me no water for my feet: but she hath washed my feet with tears, and wiped *them* with the hairs of her head. Thou gavest me no kiss: but this woman since the time I came in hath not ceased to kiss my feet. My head with oil thou didst not anoint: but this woman hath anointed my feet with ointment. Wherefore I say unto thee, Her sins, which are many, are forgiven; for she loved much: but to whom little is forgiven, *the same* loveth little" (Luke 7:44–47).

This woman loved Him dearly. She loved His reproach. She did not stop kissing His feet. A woman's glory is her hair (1 Corinthians 11:15). Feet are the least honorable part of man. Mary took her glory and wiped the dirt from His feet. She cherished His feet! If we could only worship so well. If you get the feet, you get all of Him. While the Pharisees are rebuking her with such waste, such inappropriate behavior, accusing her of being showy, she just continued to kiss His feet. Their rebukes faded with the touch and forgiveness of Jesus.

What are we most proud of? What is our glory? Is it our image? Then take our image and put it on display for God! Lay it at His feet. Is it our wealth? Pour it upon Jesus! And do it in front of the world. Let them see us giving our glory to His feet! After all, where was Jesus killed? Outside the city! That's right … not in a hospital, not in a private cathedral, but in front of the whole world. That is where God demonstrated His love for us.

Our body language says more about our love than our words do. How we act before God reveals the affections of our hearts. Men bowing before the Lord is a very powerful demonstration of giving honor to God; children are impacted by this type of devotion. The woman could have told Jesus she loved Him. After all, many people did that. However, this is the only passage where Jesus says someone demonstrated their love on Him. Not even the disciples washed His feet.

It is risky to show love for God. Like the story in Luke, the religious will rebuke us; however, Jesus will receive our love. If we would be intimate and joined to Jesus, we must leave the camp: the camp of Pentecostals, the camp of Baptists, the camp of Methodists, and the camp of Religion. Those camps do not define us; Jesus does. Camps will rob our liberty, for they will want us to blend in with the rest of the herd; they will not want us to be extravagant. Such behavior will embarrass their way of worship; therefore, leave the camp and be a fool for Christ.

Jesus left the camp. He left the camp of the Pharisees, the Sadducees, the Lawyers, and the Scribes. That is why prostitutes could touch Him and kiss His feet. That is why Jesus could openly confess His love for the sinners in front of the religious who could not understand this way of godly love.

My passion in life is Jesus Christ. Nothing and no one fulfills my longing for meaning and joy as this one person. My hunger and fascination for Jesus are all-consuming and beyond any explanation of delight! My fervor for His glory is not misplaced. I cherish His feet! I long for people to make fun of me and consider my worship to be wasteful. Give me the feet. I had rather bow before God than be raised up by men. I had rather Jesus look at me and speak to those who don't understand my love and say, "Seest thou this man? He hath washed my feet with tears, and wiped *them* with the hairs of his head. Thou gavest me no kiss: but this man hath not ceased to kiss my feet. Wherefore I say unto thee, his sins, which are many, are forgiven; for he loved much: but to whom little is forgiven, *the same* loveth little."

CHAPTER NOTES:

CHAPTER 10

On Earth As It Is In Heaven

Bowing is the response to the revelation of glory. Worship is the response to the revelation of love. How magnificent that our God is so glorious we bow and is so lovely that we worship! I want to be in a church, among people, where God is big. He is so big that small men kneel in love and reverence of this great transcendent God. When we bow before God, where are we? At His feet!

Where there is no altar, there is no throne, no correct view of God. When God is known and revealed, men bow and worship. A man with no altar is a man with no worship. There is no God in his life who "wows" him.

Let me remind you of my explanation of the word altar. When we speak of the altar, it is evident that our *altar* is always and forever the sacrifice of Jesus on the cross. Our reference to the word altar represents a place and time where believers do business with God: cry, pray, celebrate, and praise.

We believe God is here, and our hearts desire Him. We believe that He is, and we must seek Him. The altar can be anywhere in the room; however, Hebrews 13 tells us that we should **go out to Him.** "Let us go forth unto him without the camp... by Him therefore let us offer the sacrifice of praise to God continually, that is, the fruit of our lips giving thanks to His name" (Hebrews 13:13, 14).

Peter called us priests of the Lord. We are privileged to lead the worship of God. Leadership is never done in private or from the back; it is always upfront and visible. "Ye also, as lively stones, are built up a spiritual house, an holy priesthood, to offer up spiritual sacrifices, acceptable to God by Jesus Christ.... Ye are a chosen generation, a royal priesthood, an holy nation, a peculiar people; that ye should shew forth the praises of Him who hath called you out of darkness into His marvellous light" (1 Peter 2:5, 9).

We are supposed to show the praises of God. People are supposed to see us praising God, honoring God, and celebrating God. Gathering together with the particular focus of honoring and calling upon the name of the Lord is what we mean by the word altar. Call it what we will. Call it the gathering, the choir of praise, but for God's sake let the priests of the Lord show forth His praise!

The altar is where the heart can express its pursuit of God. The place where we take our shoes off, we are on holy ground. The question is not, "Why do I have to go?" but "Why would I not want to go?"

The Psalmist cried for us to come before the Lord. The Holy Spirit is compelling us to come. Coming denotes movement—movement in a particular direction and toward a desired end. Don't just come to church; come before His presence. Come before the Lord. Why would any worshiper not do this? Dead churches and dead believers do not come to altars to lead, sing, shout, dance, and praise the Lord—and the services speak for themselves—they are dead or sleeping! The priestly ministry of the saints is not functioning in these churches. There is no awareness of God's presence. The services are filled with dead faith and stale, boring confessions about a God with whom they are not impressed.

"**O COME**, let us *sing* unto the LORD: let us *make a joyful* noise to the rock of our salvation. Let us **COME BEFORE HIS PRESENCE** *with thanksgiving,* and **make a joyful** noise unto Him with psalms ... **O COME**, let us *worship* and *bow* down: let us *kneel* BEFORE THE LORD our maker" (Psalms 95:1–2, 6). Again, David commands, "**Serve** the LORD *with gladness:* **COME BEFORE HIS PRESENCE** with *singing.* Enter into his gates with thanksgiving, *and* into his courts with *praise:* **be thankful** unto him, *and* **bless** his name" (Psalms 100:2, 4).

This is how we attend church: Come and sing. Come and make a joyful noise to God. Come before Him with thanksgiving. Come and worship and bow down. Come and kneel before the Lord. Serve with gladness. Praise Him and bless His name. One thing that strikes me in these Psalms is that God is actually there. There is a conscious effort to approach or bow before the actual presence of God.

YOU BOW TO SOMETHING

Everyone has a god. There is something that captivates the heart of people. Something wows the small man. Men are created to worship. Be sure, there is an altar where men and women give their god worship. Multitudes of people who go to church are not moved by Jesus because Jesus is not their God, but they do have a god. Consider the altars of college football or whatever the popular sport is in a particular culture. Look how they dress. There is no law, no dress code, but everyone is dressed in clothing that clearly testifies their loyalty to their god. They wear their team colors. They proclaim the god's name proudly.

There is no law on how to "come," they just "come" with absolute sacrifice and energy. They do not arrive late; they actually get there very early. Hours before the event they will arrive and tailgate. They fellowship with others who love their god. Parking? No problem. They will park miles away from the stadium (church) and happily walk in rain, freezing cold, or heat to get to the stadium (church). Nothing prevents them; there are none of the typical excuses given for missing church: we had family in town, or it was too cold outside, or the weather was bad. They will sit on those metal bleachers in freezing weather or suffer in blistering heat. Rain will not deter them. For hours they will endure unpleasant climates for the celebration of their god, but never will they consider this type of commitment for Jesus. They are upset when church lasts longer than an hour. They will not come if it is raining or cold. If family is in town, Jesus will have to understand why they cannot attend. If they don't have a parking spot close to the door, then they are going home.

Oh, and the tithes they pay at the ball games! They pay their tithes up front. They buy tickets for their seats so that they are guaranteed access every week. They will then pay enormous fees to buy food and drinks. There is no law. No one is passing around an offering plate; this they do willingly. Equally, the praise is amazing. In church, for Jesus, they will sit in absolute silence. They will look with skepticism and disdain at the worship team and others who are expressing joy and love for Jesus publicly. But at the ball game, they will shout, they will scream. They will employ cheerleaders to make sure the crowd stays interested in the game. However, in church, they are so quiet, lifeless, practically dead; Jesus is not their God.

Consider the altar in a rock concert. Certainly, Satan has learned the art of worship since he was the chief worship leader in heaven before he fell. In heaven, everyone was upfront and around the altar of God. Everyone was engaged.

What is it that Satan wants? He wants to be enthroned as a god; therefore, he has implemented rock concerts (worship services) that reflect what he learned in heaven. At Satan's worship services (rock/country concerts) all the people desire to be up in front of the stage. The whole congregation is shouting, singing, and dancing with all the energy they can muster. Satan will settle for nothing less; furthermore, there is no law for people to do this—they just naturally gather at the altar of their rock star and worship with all their might. They pay extravagant tithes to buy the music, attend the worship services, wear the clothes, and evangelize others to become followers as well. But in church, they will be cold, inactive, and bored. Why? Because Jesus is not their God.

GOD IS REVERED IN HEAVEN

In heaven, the scene is much different than found in most churches. In heaven, every living thing gathers around the throne of God. The living creatures are not just sitting, standing, and watching—they are engaged in the adoration of God. In heaven, they are bowing, praising, and drawing near (surrounding) the altar of God. Should not we love God with that same intensity here on earth? Should not our worship services in church demonstrate the worth and beauty of Jesus? Should not our posture and devotion to God on earth reflect the same worship of God in heaven? Yes! Here are the scenes in heaven as recorded by John.

"The four and twenty elders **FALL DOWN BEFORE HIM** that sat on the throne, **AND WORSHIP HIM** that liveth for ever and ever, and cast their crowns before the throne, saying, Thou art worthy, O Lord, to receive glory and honour and power: for thou hast created all things, and for thy pleasure they are and were created" (Revelation 4:10–11).

"The four and twenty elders **FELL DOWN BEFORE THE LAMB** …and **THEY SUNG** a new song, saying, Thou art worthy … **SAYING WITH A LOUD VOICE**, Worthy is the Lamb that was slain to receive power, and riches, and wisdom, and strength, and honour, and glory, and blessing" (Revelation 5: 8-11). "And the four and twenty elders **FELL DOWN AND WORSHIPPED HIM** that liveth for ever and ever" (Revelation 5:14).

"The elders … **FELL BEFORE THE THRONE ON THEIR FACES, AND WORSHIPPED GOD, SAYING,** Amen: Blessing, and glory, and wisdom, and thanksgiving, and honour, and power, and might, be unto our God for ever and ever. Amen" (Revelation 7: 11-12).

And the four and twenty elders, which sat before God on their seats, **FELL UPON THEIR FACES, AND WORSHIPPED** God, **SAYING,** We give thee thanks, O Lord God Almighty, which art, and wast, and art to come;

because thou hast taken to thee thy great power, and hast reigned" (Revelation 11: 16-17).

"And after these things I heard a great voice of much people in heaven, **<u>SAYING,</u>** Alleluia; Salvation, and glory, and honour, and power, unto the Lord our God …And again **<u>THEY SAID</u>**, Alleluia… And the four and twenty elders and the four beasts **<u>FELL DOWN AND WORSHIPPED GOD</u>** that sat on the throne, saying, Amen; Alleluia." (Revelation 19:1, 3–4).

According to the whole of scripture and the demonstrative worship in heaven, our refusal to fall down on our faces before God, to kneel and worship the Lord, to loudly lift voices to Him in praise, and to cry with loud voices His worth is simple, blatant rebellion to God. It is an insult to His throne. There is no other way to reconcile the deadness of our churches other than to admit that so many who attend church do not know Jesus as God.

How can we recover our society from its rebellion and corruption if the church cannot restore worship? If the church cannot demonstrate the heavenly worship in our churches, how will we demonstrate the Kingdom of God in our earthly institutions? Our refusal to worship God, our refusal to praise God the way the Bible commands us, is nothing but rebellion.

If we want God's kingdom on earth as it is in heaven, we have to do the things they are doing in heaven. BOWING down before the Lord AND WORSHIPING IS THE NORM IN HEAVEN. In heaven, there is no argument over whether bowing is part of the culture. It is kingdom culture! If the saints on earth would join the saints in heaven in the worship of our great King, the earth would reel from the influence of that heavenly kingdom. Kingdoms of darkness would be exposed and humiliated. Bondage and addictions would be broken. The enemy's strongholds in our society would be dismantled. The absolute moral confusion, social division, and political corruption would be completely exposed and corrected.

If there is any hope for our civilization, we must submit our culture to His culture regardless of our traditions. This type of worship is not out of compulsion or law, it is the freewill offering of those who have a revelation of the glory and love of Jesus. We do not have to force people who love Jesus to do this anymore than we have to force a person at a rock concert to go up front and sing, dance, and shout. It is the nature of worship. If Jesus is the God one worships, then this is the way their life will demonstrate His worth.

DON'T TEXT ABOUT SERIOUS ISSUES

I do not like to counsel on the phone. I do not like to express my feelings to my loved ones over the phone or through texting. I like to look them in the face. When I counsel, I prefer to be face-to-face looking into the eyes of the people before me and looking into their souls. So much can be seen and known by a person's body language.

For centuries, God has communicated what He desires of us. "… this people draw near me with their mouth, and with their lips do honour me, but have removed their heart far from me …" (Isaiah 29:13). God wants the love of our hearts more than the religious exercise of a worship service. God wants our heart to draw near to Him. It is not enough for God that we get our bodies to the church and sing a few songs yet all the while our hearts are far from Him.

God wants our whole selves in worship. David knew this. "Bless the Lord, O my soul: and **ALL** that is within me …" (Psalms 103:1). Our actions speak louder than words. God is not going to believe we love Him because we say we do. He wants our hearts. Praise is the body's expression of the heart's joy in the Lord. David commanded his whole self to bless the Lord. David's whole self was an instrument of worship to God. Our bodies are instruments of worship. Our bodies have percussion instruments, string instruments, wind instruments, and volume; we can produce harmonies and keep beats. If we would offer our whole selves to God and honor God on earth as they do in heaven, we would see heaven intrude on the helpless state of our present world.

Please don't let dry men, though full of devotion, explain to you passionate affection for God! We have been trained to worship God by a fallen emotionally crippled culture. Stoic men and women who cannot even express love to their spouses and children want to tell us how to love God? I don't think so! American men are uncomfortable with public displays of affection, and European men are the same—they are too proud to express their feelings.

I want to be affectionate with God. I want a big God who astounds me and causes my heart to rapture with delight. I want to fall before Him on my face, and I want everyone to see! God has very openly and publicly displayed His affection for me; I shall do likewise. This strange rebellious excuse to not worship God as they do in heaven has been culturally created by a corrupt religion. What ministers have done to worship is inexcusable and indefensible.

Beloved, don't follow tradition; follow the Spirit. Don't be bound to a religious culture, but let us join ourselves to that heavenly world. As it is in heaven so let it be on earth.

CHAPTER NOTES:

CHAPTER 11

Make Jesus Happy

Love is of God, and only lovers can know God, for "everyone that loveth is born of God and knoweth God" (1 John 4:7). God is love. Love makes the ultimate sacrifice to win those who would destroy themselves. Love gives and sacrifices so others can live. God loves even when He is not loved. God gives even when He is not asked to give. God paid the debt when the slaves asked to be left alone. God loved us. God sent His Son to us. God made His Son the propitiation for our sins.

In his book *The Knowledge of the Holy*, A.W. Tozer wrote, "You have declared Your unchanging love for us in Christ Jesus. If nothing in us can win Your love, nothing in the universe can prevent You from loving us. Your love is uncaused and undeserved. You are Yourself the reason for love."

Love casts out fear, and our troubled hearts are given peace. A.W. Tozer went on to say, "Because God is self-existent, His love had no beginning; because He is eternal, His love can have no end; because He is infinite, it has no limit; because He is holy, His love is the epitome of all spotless purity; because He is immense, His love is incomprehensibly vast, bottomless, a shoreless sea before which we kneel in joyful silence and from which the loftiest eloquence retreats confused and abashed."

Love wills the good of all and never desires harm or evil to any. Oh joyful religion where it is the duty of man, the high calling of man, to love—to love because God is love. The man who loves abides in God and God in him. How vastly set apart is the faith of Christians from all others; theirs is a God of joy, peace, and love. The screams and abuses of those outside of Christ belong to those who worship gods other than Jesus. Listen to the devil's music. It is all about pain, sex, abuse, drugs, and depression—the screaming lyrics, the brutal abuse upon the body. But look at the worship of God. The glory. The celebrations. The joy. The happiness. Blessed religion indeed, where it is the command to be joyful, to have peace, and to rejoice.

Jesus was happy. Why? Because He was the full, final, and perfect expression of the Father. The Father is happy. The Holy Spirit is happy. How do I know? I know because Hebrews 1:9 declares that God has anointed Jesus with the oil of gladness. The anointing of the Holy Spirit on Jesus was gladness. The Holy Spirit is glad. The Father is glad.

What does this mean? What is the message about gladness? Gladness means extreme joy—the feeling of joy, the experience of delight, and uninhibited happiness. Jesus was anointed with extreme joy and gladness. How? Why? Because He loved righteousness and hated iniquity; therefore, God anointed Him with the oil of gladness above all other men. That's right. No one who has ever lived experienced and possessed more uninhibited happiness than Jesus because He loved righteousness. How foolish are those who pursue the devil's deceits and think happiness is in this world or in one's possessions.

Jesus was anointed with gladness. To anoint means to consecrate Jesus to the Messianic office and to furnish Him with the necessary powers for its administration. The book of Hebrews tells us, "Who for the joy that was set before him, endured the cross ..." (Hebrews 12:2). What was that joy waiting beyond the cross? Indeed, some of it had to be the knowledge that His death would bring many sons into glory. God and man would be reconciled. The longing and loving heart of the Father would have the rapturous delight of enjoying love with His once-wayward children. Jesus' soul would be made an offering for sin, and by Jesus God would justify many. This was a portion, if not all, of Jesus' gladness.

The joy of Jesus is not in His power to condemn the wicked but in forgiving them and putting their sins away. His love was His anointing to usher in the New Covenant whereby God could make the wicked righteous and the Holy God could have intimacy with those who were once rebels. Luke describes Jesus' anointing like this: "The Spirit of the Lord *is* upon me, because he hath anointed me to preach the gospel to the poor; he hath sent me to heal the brokenhearted, to preach deliverance to the captives, and recovering of sight to the blind, to set at liberty them that are bruised, to preach the acceptable year of the Lord" (Luke 4:18–19).

We can see the gladness of Jesus. It was in His ability to help the broken, the sinner, the destitute, the lost, the incurable, and the wretched. It was His ability to make the wicked righteous, for He loves righteousness! It was in His ability to bring many sons and daughters into glory and give His beloved Father such delight; He would be the answer to His Father's longings.

JESUS IS EXTREMELY JOYFUL WHEN HE GETS TO SHOW GRACE AND MERCY

Jesus is extremely joyful when He gets to show grace and mercy by pardoning, saving, and healing the unrighteous. Though He loves righteousness, He does not hate the unrighteous. Just as His love is not like our love, His hate is not like our hate. As a father may hate the illness destroying his son, the father loves his son all the more. So, Jesus hates what unrighteousness is doing to His creation, but loves the unrighteous all the more. His love is so deep that He would go to war with their unrighteousness and destroy every trace of their sin and rebellion against the Holy Father; this makes Him glad. How unhappy Jesus would be if He loved the unrighteous but had no power to help them. However, He does have power. The Spirit of the Lord is upon Him, and He can help them. He is anointed to remove their sin.

When Jehoshaphat went to war, he sent the tribe of praise out before the army declaring, "… His mercy endures forever!" Psalms 136 has twenty-six verses, and the Psalm calls for praise twenty-six times because, "His mercy endures forever." I seriously think God is trying to tell us something about His mercy—it endures forever!

What is mercy? Mercy is loving kindness. It is the constant of God. The thing that endures forever in God is not His wrath, but His mercy. Forever God is demonstrating His loving kindness. This teaches us the very thing Satan does not want us to know. Satan wants us to think that God is like all the other gods—He is angry, He is difficult to please, He is tight-fisted, He is so frustrated with you. However, God has revealed the very opposite. God has declared that He is not to be trifled with. He is the judge. He is holy. He will judge the wicked. He will pour His wrath upon sin, but He has made a way of escape. He has made provision for the wicked and the sinner.

God does not want the wicked to perish, nor does He enjoy judging them. What makes God happy is His ability to pardon sinners. God leaves you with that choice: to receive His pardon or His wrath. Jesus is not frustrated when we come to Him for forgiveness. He is not angry when we bring our sins to Him. He is offended when we don't!

When did you ever see Jesus angry at having to forgive a sinner? Instead, He was always exceedingly happy to do so. Jesus even revealed that all the angels in heaven rejoice (as though a grand party is thrown in heaven) whenever one sinner repents. Jesus loves to put sin away, not the sinner. Jesus loves to forgive the wicked. Jesus loves to give righteousness to those who believe Him; He loves it; and the more sinners to whom He imparts righteousness, the happier He is; He loves righteousness.

SO MUCH HAPPENED AT THE CROSS

I pray this will help us see that there's more to the cross of Jesus than people usually see. Jesus was not a victim on that cross—He was a lamb! The Lamb. He was a soldier destroying Satan's hold on your life. He was the Truth exposing the lies about our heavenly Father. He was a King destroying the devil's kingdom. He was the way-maker to open heaven's gates for all who will come. Jesus didn't die out of pity. The cross is the expression of who God is! The cross reveals the kind of love God has. He would die on a cross before letting us die in our sins.

Furthermore, the cross is how the Father can forever fulfill His intense longing to show His everlasting mercy and grace to us. When Jesus sees us turning to Him, His mercies erupt within His heart. He bursts with gladness. This is illustrated in the parable of the prodigal son. The prodigal's father was so glad his son came home; he was ecstatic that the son who was dead was now alive.

Jesus is not tired of us; that is why He is our High Priest. He ever lives to make intercession for us. He can save to the uttermost those who come to God by Him because He lives forever. Jesus is not tired of us. He is not tired of our failings. He is not resentful that we need forgiveness. The Bible assures just the opposite is true. Whenever we come to God, agree with God about our lives and our sins, He is faithful and just to forgive us and cleanse us of all unrighteousness; He loves righteousness.

It is Satan who wants us to think God is tired of us. What breaks the heart of God is when we don't come to Him—when we mistrust His grace and kind heart by thinking we are too bad to seek God. It offends God when you try to clean up our sins (which we can never do) for He is the One who is anointed to save us from our sins.

If we are suffering from despair over our struggle with sin, be confident that Jesus is not. Though we may be very grieved over our inability to overcome strongholds, Jesus is still glad. He is glad because there is not a sinner He cannot save. There is not a bondage He cannot break. The Lord Jesus commands every situation; the most challenging and unruly actions rob none of His gladness. He can perfect those who trust Him—this makes Him glad.

Jesus is not afraid of our sin; He soundly conquered it through His cross. Jesus runs into the world of unrighteous people with compassion flooding His heart and gladness bursting through His eyes, for He is mighty to save. Jesus, the glad One, has come to rob unrighteousness of its claims and make all men righteous.

I call us to worship this Jesus. I urge us to overcome our temptations to despair. Yes, we may suffer sadness over our struggles, but Jesus is glad. He is not glad we are sad; He is not glad we are suffering; He is not glad that we sin; He is glad that He can save us.

I long to emphasize the ability of God. I am coming to those who have wandered away from God. I am coming to the ones Satan has overthrown. I am coming to those who are in the ruin of sin. I am coming to those whose hearts condemn them—those whom Satan would seek to destroy. I am coming to us, imploring us to not give up on Jesus. Worship Him. Don't throw away our confidence, which has great recompense of reward. Worship the glad Savior. Cry out to Jesus to not give up on us.

Have we grown tired of the church and religion? Are we humiliated by the lack of heart or ability to live holy lives? Do we constantly fail? There is hope for us. Worship Jesus with a faith that believes He is able even when we are not. Go ahead, let's give up on ourselves; call ourselves unworthy; but understand that God anoints Jesus to minister our salvation and give us the righteousness of God.

We may be going through hell right now, but Jesus is praying for us; therefore, we don't have to live in the shame of our past or the destruction of sin. We don't have to be haunted by shame and loss. Everyone has something they are deeply ashamed of, hoping they never get found out. Don't let this fear keep us from the One who will gladly save us. God offers new lives where past sins have no more power.

GOD'S MESSAGE TO THE BACKSLIDER

If we are tempted to believe that God is tired of us, we need to hear what God said. If we think that God is disgusted with us, then we need to stop listening to our emotions and Satan's lies, and listen to God. The Lord says, "Turn, O backsliding children … for I am married unto you …" (Jeremiah 3:14). Can we believe God is saying this to us? He is! Face the cross. Consider that it is there on that cross where God gave His life for us! Now try to convince me that He does not love us.

So how do we turn to God? We have come so many times only to sink back into failure. Those are all our testimonies. That was Paul's testimony. That was Peter's testimony. But this is the God who forgives not once … not twice … not even three times, but seventy times seven times, and then again.

Are we scared to turn to God? Are we ashamed of our constant failings? I understand. But we must worship Jesus and not our ability to perfect ourselves. We must do what God says to do and not follow our emotions or intellectual reasonings, for God's ways are not our ways, nor or His thoughts our thoughts. Here is what God says we should do, "… return unto the LORD thy God; for thou hast fallen by thine iniquity. Take with you words, and turn to the LORD: say unto him, take away all iniquity, and receive *us* graciously: so will we render the calves of our lips. Asshur shall not save us; we will not ride upon horses: neither will we say any more to the work of our hands, *Ye are* our gods: for in thee the fatherless findeth mercy" (Hosea 14:1–3). God responds to this worship by declaring, "I will heal their backsliding, I will love them freely: for mine anger is turned away from him" (Hosea 14:4).

How long will we refuse a God so tender and compassionate? We may have nothing good ... absolute shame and filth are all we have left. We are overwhelmed with unworthiness, but all God asks us to bring is words. Do we have words? He even tells us what to say! Oh, what a glad God. Just take with us our words. What are we waiting for?

Understand what makes Jesus glad. "Return, thou backsliding Israel and I will not cause my anger to fall upon you: for I am merciful and I will not keep anger forever. Only acknowledge thine iniquity, that thou has transgressed against the Lord thy God ... and ye have not obeyed my voice ... Turn, O backsliding children ... for I am married unto you" (Jeremiah 3: 12-14).

Jesus is glad is when He lets go of His wrath and shows mercy instead. All He wants us to do is acknowledge our sin. He does not ask us to stop sinning because that power only comes from Him. He does not ask us to clean ourselves up before we come to Him because He alone can cleanse us. He simply asks us to acknowledge our sin and turn to Him; then He can let go of His anger and cause it not to fall on us.

Jesus is not glad that we suffer. Our suffering is the result of our rebellion against Him. All of us went astray from God. We teamed up with Satan and stood against the Lord. We became slaves to the devil. It is Satan who has tormented us. He has abused us and has stolen so much from us. Satan likes to make you think that all these problems are because of God. He would like to get in our heads and tell us, "Well, if God is love, then why is He allowing you to suffer like this?" Or, "If God is good, if God is love, then why do innocent children suffer?"

All humanity suffers because we have rebelled against God and chosen to follow Satan. God has come to our rescue and desires to restore our lives and joy. Jesus comes with gladness because He has the unmatched power to conquer Satan soundly and destroy his rule over our lives. All Jesus needs us to do is turn to Him, acknowledge our sin, and bring our words to Him. Jesus will heal us. Jesus will gladly set us free.

Jesus hates what Satan and sin have done to us. Because Jesus loves us, He came to us. Even when we hated Jesus, He still came to us in love. Jesus came to do something about what happened to us. He hates what has happened to us and has come to put an end to these abuses. He hates what we have suffered. He hates our loneliness. He hates our orphan spirit. He hates the toll disease has taken on our bodies. He hates the fear that torments us. He hates what our abuse has done to us. So, the Creator has come to make us new. One cry out of us and Jesus comes running—He cannot help it; He loves us! "Bless the LORD, O my soul, and forget not all his benefits: Who forgiveth all thine iniquities; who healeth all thy diseases; Who redeemeth thy life from destruction; who crowneth thee with lovingkindness and tender mercies" (Psalms 103:3–4).

CHAPTER NOTES:

CHAPTER 12

What Is Jesus Like?

L ook up into the heavens and behold who has created these things. Gaze into the cosmos, the unsearchable and insatiable powers of the ether, and behold the power of Him who created it all.

The God who made the world and everything in it—He is Lord of heaven and earth. He is not sustained by those things which sustain us. He derives no increase from those things which He has made. He is not upheld by the things that uphold us. God has made everything by the power of His Word. From nothing and out of nothing, He has created all things. Nothing exists apart from Him, and by His Word He upholds all things.

He is transcendent from all things created. He is invisible, yet manifest. He is everywhere distant, yet intimately close. There is nothing that is which is like unto Him! His nature is made from nothing. He is Spirit, and they who worship Him can only worship Him in Spirit and truth.

Few have chased after Him. Most have lived unaware and unconcerned. Like children playing in the puddles of a shore when before them is all the ocean's depth, men have concerned themselves with origins and not the Originator. We trifle with such unspectacular inventions when the Uncreated is all around us being revealed and disclosed. But we are occupied with building a better toy. Perhaps we try to build a better telescope to discover something about the dirt on Saturn when the Incomprehensible, Unfathomable, Self-existent One is waiting for someone to believe that He is.

Yes, send the telescopes into space but not to examine dirt—discover the Creator! Stand in awe of His power. The heavens declare Thy glory, Lord. And Jesus said, "Blessed are the pure in heart, for they shall see God" (Matthew 5:8).But how shall we see Him? By what perception? Who or what shall help us see Him who is invisible?

Robbed of sight, few have allowed their hearts to be fascinated with the wonder of God. Fewer still have entered an experience with Him by which they are mightily enraptured with the transcendence of God. Just look at how few in the church drop to their knees in His presence. The majority stand with boredom and flesh out the songs of the Most High God, and for this we are now paying too heavy a price. As the book of Romans declares, they changed the image of the incorruptible God into an image like men and animals. They did not like to retain God in their thoughts, but instead worshiped and served the creature rather than the creator. For this cause, God handed them over to a reprobate mind to live and practice things that are destructive to the constitution of civilization's sanity. Mass confusion is the natural result of a people who abandon the Living God for the demon gods they had rather serve. This false worship has produced a world of moral confusion, gender confusion, spiritual confusion, and political confusion.

Is there an answer to this ruin? Yes! Restore the worship of the True and Living God.

God is not a good idea. He is necessary. Nothing else works apart from Him. No creature has life in itself; all life is a gift from God. Man is nothing without God. Without God, man falls apart. Man is not original; his genius is less than elementary compared to the vast ethos of God's brilliance. Man has nothing to say. If he does say anything worthwhile, then at that point he is simply an echo of the original Word.

How can we know Him? How can we see Him? What is He like? Who can show us God? Various reports have been told of missionaries seeing Hindu worshipers tapping on trees and stones and whispering, "Are you there?" to the god they hoped might reside within. But God did not come in the trees and stones. The Word became flesh and dwelt among us. We beheld His glory—the glory as the one and only Son from the Father, full of grace and truth (John 1).

He walked among us: present, near to everything, near to us, entering into our suffering, bearing our pain, and taking our sins. God drew near to us in the person of His Son Jesus, and Jesus lives to bring us near to God, to wake us up and give us eyes to see the invisible God. Jesus is the invisible God made visible. Jesus is the transcendent God made knowable. Paul ascribes that He, Jesus, is the image of the invisible God. All things have been created through him, and unto him; and he is before all things, and in him all things consist (Col 1:15–17).

Furthermore, the scriptures testify that "God ... Hath in these last days spoken unto us by his Son ... by whom also he made the worlds; Who being the brightness of his glory, and the express image of His person, and upholding all things by the word of his power …" (Hebrews 1:1–3).

WHAT DID JESUS SHOW US?

What did Jesus show us? What did Jesus bring us? What was revealed in Jesus? What, in the person of Jesus, was manifested in flesh concerning God's heart? Jesus manifested God's love. John said in his gospel, "… we have seen his glory, glory as of the only Son from the Father, full of grace and truth … For from his fullness we have all received, grace upon grace. For the law was given through Moses; grace and truth came through Jesus Christ. No one has ever seen God; the only God, who is at the Father's side, he has made him known" (John 1:14,16–18 ESV).

How did Jesus make the Father knowable? By giving us grace for grace, by offering us His fullness, His life, by showing that the true understanding of God is that He is full of grace and truth! Furthermore, those who receive this love are not worthy of it. John said the Father manifested His heart by giving Jesus to us and loving us when we did not love Him. "In this the love of God was made manifest among us, that God sent his only Son into the world, so that we might live through him. In this is love, not that we have loved God but that he loved us and sent his Son to be the propitiation for our sins" (1 John 4:9–10 ESV).

The God we see in Jesus is benevolent, kind, and forgiving toward His enemies—One who is willing to humble Himself to extend forgiveness. But wait, not only willing to humble Himself, but also willing to sacrifice Himself so that His enemies can live. Jesus had rather He died on a cross than let you die in your sins. This is the way God wants to glorify Himself.

Man's glory is normally thought to lie in his ability to exalt himself and humble others to his will. "That is glory, that is power," says the world. Glory in a man's eyes is always that which exalts himself. However, in Jesus, we see that God's glory consists in the very opposite. God's glory and power are revealed in His grace and truth. God sought to reveal His heart by humbling Himself (Philippians 2) and saving His enemies. Any god can cause the weak to tremble before their power and awe, but Jesus revealed His glory by His willingness to humble Himself for the sake of man. He would not reveal His heart by a mighty display of power that would break in pieces those who oppose Him, but by hiding that power and showing grace to the undeserving as they turn to Him in repentance.

THE INFINITELY DESIRABLE GOD

Here, in Jesus, is a revelation of God that makes Him not only understandable but also infinitely desirable. Might and power would make Him fearfully terrible, but **goodness, grace, love, forgiveness, healing, saving, friendship, and fathering** is what makes Him INFINITELY DESIRABLE. This glory is seen not in God's ability to threaten, bully, and judge, but in His ability to heal, forgive, and comfort. This **Grace** is a shining aspect of God's glory!

Of all the accusations hurled at Jesus, no one ever accused Him of not loving them. Nobody walked away from Jesus saying, "I wonder what God is like?" Do they walk away from our churches saying, "I wonder what Jesus is like?" As Jesus was the witness of the Father, the church is the witness of Jesus. Man's potential is to reflect the uncreated Light. We are not that Light but a reflection. If there was no Light, there would be no us! And we are not that Voice, but a mouthpiece of that Voice. Take that Voice away and we have nothing to say. The church is the object upon which Jesus can manifest Himself.

Look at the darkness of space. Light is there, but it has nothing to shine upon. Objects give glory to light as light gives glory to objects. Take away light and a rose is no longer beautiful. Your beauty is derived from the light shining upon you. Jesus was the object upon which His Father could shine and manifest His essence. The church is that object upon which Jesus can shine in order that He may be revealed on the earth. People should look at us and see Christ. They should see grace and truth. Paul said the Kingdom of God is in righteousness, peace, and joy in the Holy Ghost. That is what the reflection of Jesus should be through us. The church should make Jesus infinitely desirable.

Those living behind the cloak of religious piety, who have no grace, want us to live in tears and sorrow. They would constantly remind us of our corruption, demanding we live in a state of humiliation. Is this really the worship God wants?

Are we a reflection of the true Light? If people want to be like Jesus but don't want to be like us, then something is wrong with our revelation of Jesus. If people can't fellowship with us because we are too holy, then we are unlike Christ and our spirituality is poison! According to the scriptures, the worship that truly honors God is the worship of a joyful heart because the Lord is their God. "Blessed are the people whose God is the LORD!" (Psalms 144:15 ESV).

But these religious joy-robbers are so unfamiliar with Jesus. They are so far from the love of God. They are constantly presenting a god that nobody wants to worship or be close to.

They not only change the image of the incorruptible God, but they change His message. It is as though the words of Jesus have been changed into "And all men will know you are my disciples by your AGONY, YOUR CONSTANT TEARS OF REPENTANCE, YOUR WAILING OVER YOUR SHORT-COMINGS!" Such an attitude conveys the idea that the Kingdom of God is religion, turmoil, and agony in the Holy Ghost.

I believe when the Lord is among His people, there ought to be a shout of triumph. The King is in our midst; let the people rejoice! Yes, we cry and repent, but is there not fruit from that sowing? Should we not rejoice in the Father who forgives us? Shall we not find joy in the Father who loves us and gives us hope? Is it wrong to enjoy JOY when the King has delivered us and guaranteed our provision of freedom?

MAKE JESUS INFINITELY DESIRABLE

Seek only to be an expression of Jesus. Rely fully upon the grace of God. Live in the Holy Spirit. Walk in the Spirit. Commune with the Holy Spirit. He is the great possibility. By Him and through Him, believers can manifest the worthy demonstration of Jesus in the world.

Don't hide the joy. Lavish forgiveness upon the sinner. Be extravagant with the love of God. Give it everywhere, especially where it is not welcomed. Preach hope to the hopeless. Go after the suffering. Welcome the rejected and outcast. Suffer all for Him. Take every occasion as an opportunity to manifest what He is indeed like.

If we get hit with abuse, let Jesus come out of us. Don't hide our true selves behind the cloak of religious piety. This hypocrisy stinks to high heaven. Be real. Be raw. Let people see us walk in failure, pain, success, and joy. Let them see it all! Don't be afraid of our weakness as though it is something we must hide lest someone discover that we are not perfect. Our ability to admit our weakness is our strength, for then grace and glory rest upon us.

When we fail to reveal Christ, then sincerely repent; get up and walk on so that others may see what a good Father He is to us. Here is a newsflash—everyone knows we are not perfect. God only had one good Son, and we are not Him.

I am so hungry for a true baptism of holiness. Not religious holiness, but the kind where I am finished with self. Where I have no reputation to defend. A holiness that has produced a pure heart that sees God and not wretches everywhere!

So here is my thesis. What does a man look like who has been saved by the blood of another? What does a man look like who has not gotten what he deserved but infinitely better?

What does mercy draped over a sinner look like? What does the passion to love God look like in a man who discovers how deep God loves him? What does the passion look like and feel like in a heart that has been given hope? How does this person live? How does he look? What is he like? What does the spiritual man look like? Is he jovial or stern? Happy or sad? Inviting or scary?

What does the man look like who has just been rescued by the grace of God? Imagine the attitude of a man who has been consoled by God's gospel of grace assuring him, "I will never remember your sins again. I will never leave you nor forsake you. I am coming again to get you so you can be with me forever—IN PARADISE. I will not leave you comfortless; I will come to you and comfort you. I want you to be with me and see the glory I had with the Father before the world began.

No weapon formed against you shall prosper. I give you peace beyond understanding. I will deliver you from every bondage. I will fight for you against every enemy. When you pass through the fire, you will not be burned. When you pass through the water, you will not drown. I will heal all your diseases. I will direct your paths. I will give you power. I will feed you. I will not let you be condemned. By love, I will deliver you from all fear. I will put no conditions on my love for you. I will perfect all that concerns you. When you are in trouble, I will be your help. I will be your shepherd. I will lead you beside still waters. I will restore your soul. I will let angels camp all around you for protection. I will comfort you in all your sorrow. I will give you joy for mourning. I will be your shield. No good thing will I withhold from you. I will marry you."

Would this man be the most merciful man we have ever met? Would he be kind and patient? Would he be joyful? When he is sad, would he not have a place to run to?

I'd rather live my life as a fool, believing the New Covenant Gospel than hold any other belief! The religion that men and devils have concocted provides no reason to live and no hope to go on. Only God could come up with something so truly fantastic as Christianity. What is Jesus like? He is astounding! He is transcendently glorious. He is like nothing else. He is like no one else. There is not another like Him—not anywhere; never has been, never will be.

CHAPTER NOTES:

CHAPTER 13

Just One Look Changed Everything

Many years ago, I remember reading of a minister who was intent on worshiping God with his whole life. He suffered greatly from his failure and the constant distractions that he battled as he pursued God in worship. Hearing of an aged minister who enjoyed joyful intimacy with God, he sought the man out for assistance. He contacted the aged and respected minister whose life exemplified worship to inquire about a particular time of instruction.

He asked the aged man, "What is it like to be with God—to truly worship God?" The old man responded, "While you are with me, we will spend our time together. I will teach you all that is possible, everything I know. However, I cannot teach you experience. There will come a point when you hear a call from deep within; it is imperative that you give complete diligence to that call. If you do, you will experience the worship of God!"

The aged worshiper of God told the young man, "You will meet with me at all my appointed times of prayer."

Several times during the day, the two men would go off to pray and shut themselves in with God. Indeed, the young man was stirred by the intimacy the aged worshiper had with God and sought with great effort to have the same. However, the harder he tried the more complex the most common spiritual exercises became.

Unable to sleep, the young man began fumbling around the house in the early morning hours. He noticed a light in the study. Gazing through the opening in the door, he saw the aged worshiper holding the globe in his arms as though he were hugging it. The old man's tears were flowing, hitting the globe and running all over the world. The young man said that he learned more about worship at that moment than he had in all the days of his life.

He realized that worship has nothing to do with the energy of the flesh and trying harder to succeed. It is not the routine of religious exercises, but the surrender of a heart to the fire of God! It is something that happens because we walk with Jesus. However, the young man was discouraged because he feared his heart would never be as receptive as the old man's.

The next day, the weather turned bad. It was rainy as the storms rolled through. After attending to a few duties in town the young man returned to see the aged worshiper, but he was not home. He discovered that the man was down in his office. So off he went to seek out the old man. By the time he got to the man's office in the center of town, he could hear the aged minister. He could hear him singing. He sang the lines from that great hymn, "Come Thou Fount of Every Blessing." The young man stood alone in the darkness and the rain, listening … pondering the truth he had heard.

Prone to wander, Lord, I feel it,
Prone to leave the God I love.
Here's my heart, o, take and seal it,
Seal it for Thy courts above.

As he stood outside, seeing the flicker of the candle in his room, he felt he was standing on sacred soil. The old man's private worship was obvious. He walked away having learned that worship was not an event, not an exercise, nor was it a discipline. Worship was intimacy with a real and Living God. Worship is not what we do; it is what we are. People worship publicly because they worship privately.

The young man listened as the aged worshiper gave his heart to God all over again as though it were the first time he had ever met Jesus. The young man could sense the urgency of the old man's cry. The thing the old man feared more than anything was a cold heart! The young man pondered on the idea that this aged worshiper of God was not worshiping God because he was a great worshiper but because God is a great God. The old man feared his heart and did the only thing with it he knew to do; he gave his heart to God—every day!

The young man spoke with his mentor and confessed that he overheard him praying in the early morning and now at the office. He then said to the old man, "You told me all the times you prayed, but you didn't tell me about these other times. The aged worshiper said, "One thing you've got to learn about God if you want to have a fiery baptism of His Spirit: make appointments with God, and always keep them." The old man continued, "Son, every time you and I prayed together that was my appointment with the Father, but those other times of prayer were the Father's appointment with me! When He called me in that morning hour, my heart said, "Your face, oh God, will I seek."

How are our hearts? Can we hear God calling for us? Do we answer? Is the deep in us crying back to God? Do we lie awake on our beds at night longing for Him? Have we heard Him longing for us? Do we respond? Have we discovered that everything we are looking for in life—everything we want for happiness—is in the Lord?

A.W. Tozer commented in his book *The Pursuit Of God*, "Let the average man be put to the proof on the question of who is above, and his true position will be exposed. Let him be forced into making a choice between God and money, between God and men, between God and personal ambition, God and self, God and human love, and God will take second place every time. Those other things will be exalted above. However the man may protest, the proof is in the choices he makes day after day throughout his life."

JESUS IS TRANSCENDENT

Jesus is supernaturally unmatched, unequaled, and unrivaled. He is supremely above all other things. He is beyond comparison. Nothing can be brought up or presented that can even pose a worthy distraction. Jesus is astounding. He gripped the hearts of people from all walks of life.

Since the time of His arrival on earth, multitudes have flocked to Him. From every race, people, tribe, and tongue they have surrendered their hearts to Him. He is not a passing fad. He is not a fairy tale. He is the center of all history. He is the image of the invisible God. To be stunned by Jesus is to be stunned by God.

Do not be fooled by some mere professors. Multitudes believe in Him but have never been arrested by His worth. They have no capacity to perceive the excellencies of the Lord. God's love surpasses all human emotion and intellect. Seeing and grasping the unfathomable God demands a spiritual hunger and capacity that only the Spirit of the Lord can provide.

Bland people who gather to listen to the Bible being preached, who sit in pews without emotion, who sing songs to a God their hearts have never met, are not to be confused with those worshipers who have stolen away from the allurements of disciplines and formalities and pressed their way into the Divine presence and passionately cry to Him, "I heard you! My heart heard you. You said to seek your face. Here I am Lord. My heart wants to seek your face."

Multitudes through the years have given Him their lives, hearts, and worship. They forsook fortunes and fame to know Him. Great men followed Jesus. Men who changed history and sired nations followed Jesus. They were eyewitnesses of His majesty. Worship God … and enjoy Him—this is the sole duty of man.

The heart is the primary issue: all God has wanted and sought in man was a burning heart of love. Jesus said the most significant thing a man can do is to love the Lord with all his heart, strength, and mind. If a man does not worship God, he is broken. His world is broken!

CAN WE WORSHIP JESUS?

Jesus is the hero of heaven, the hero of the ages, the hero of the church, but is He yours? The proof is in the pudding. Notice the number of depressed people who go to church. They do not worship God. They sing. They have respect, but they refuse to give Him their worship publicly. They choose depression over praise.

God does not have many friends and lovers. Jesus questioned Peter asking if he loved Him more than "these things." These things refer to religion. Do we love Jesus or His miracles? Do we love Jesus or how He feeds the poor? Do we love Jesus or His teachings on love? Jesus asks us today, "Do you love Me more than the hymns, the church, the ministry?"

Many want Jesus in their homes and like having Him near, but they do not lie awake in their beds and think about Him through the night. Many like to go to the house of God and have Jesus as the guest of honor. Like all the men at Simon the leper's house, they love to sit around and have Jesus entertain them, but how few are the Marys who break their alabaster boxes and pour upon Him their unashamed love?

God is the great lover. We think we are the ones pursuing God, but the truth is that He is the One pursuing us. There is a love that is better than life! Think of it! God is delighting in you—LOVING YOU. For this love, men and women of all ages have stolen away from the world's allurements to saturate themselves in absolute delight. They were the happiest people on the planet! People like Paul considered the value of all the world's goods and attainments as dung compared to the beauty of Jesus Christ! What did they know? They knew Him. They were eyewitnesses of His majesty. They saw Him. They beheld

His glory. They did not follow cunning fables; they gave their lives for someone!

Come on now! Do we want to be great? I hear it all the time, "I want to do something great. I want my life to count." Well, here is the greatest thing we can do ... the greatest! Love the Lord our God with all our heart! That is right. The greatest thing is not how much money we give, not how many mission trips we take, not how often we fast, or how popular we are at preaching. All too often, these things become the things we love, and God is lost to our godly endeavors. Why is this so hard to understand?

I was the guest speaker at a pastor's conference in Warsaw, Poland. I spoke on this subject of worship—of having our passions set on fire for God with all our affections erupting within us for Him. One morning, an aged pastor approached me. He was sarcastic—full of religion and dryness—saying, "You know this is not true; it is impossible to have such affections with God, such emotions."

I asked him, "Have you ever kissed God? Have you ever heard Him sing over you? Have you ever touched Him? Has He ever kissed you?" He said, "I do not understand." I held his hand and said, "You poor, poor preacher!" Then I walked away.

The next day he sought me out weeping and asked, "Is it possible?" I said, "What kind of God would offer His Son as a sacrifice for my life and would not want to be intimate with me?" He said, "I am different. I believe. I shall love Him with my heart and soul!"

A few days later, the look in his eyes was different; his worship was different. I approached him. He said, "I have something to tell you." I replied, "You already did." He said, "But we have not spoken for a few days." To which I agreed, but

I was able to tell him that I have seen that you now see. Your worship is different; your eyes are different—you look like a man who has been in the secret place. Elated, he responded with tears and smiles. His weeping prevented him from speaking clearly, but he did manage to say that it is true: God is to be loved and our hearts are to be afire.

THE FIGHT OF FAITH

If we want an enduring ministry, never lose the sense of wonder and glory in the cross and blood of Jesus—consider it the most spectacular display of love and beauty that cannot be improved.

The fight of faith and the battle to behold the glory of the Lord is a day-to-day fight. Sometimes, this must be a violent act of faith. I mean violent in the sense of pursuit. The fight of faith is not allowing our sight or feelings to distract us from what is real. By faith, we overcome the demands of lesser things for the reward of the Irreplaceable One. We must, by faith, believe and act upon the promise that He is a Rewarder!

A.W. Tozer explained it like this, "I would rather die, I would rather walk out here on the sidewalk and drop over and be gathered up by the authorities and carried away than to lose my receptivity and lose my hunger and lose my DISCONTENT WITH MY PRESENT STATE. No longing after God, no deep yearning for holiness, no inner hunger to be like Jesus!"

Please don't let dry men full of devotion, RUINED BY SEMINARIES, explain to you passionate affection for God! These drab people, destitute of the Holy Ghost and fire, DRAB MINISTERS who have institutionalized the church and know nothing of worship may give me a lesson in Hebrew, but they know nothing about the secret place. The tragedy of the ages: The God of love, who sacrificially pursues man with perfect love, is scorned by the man. The tragedy in the church: dry men, who lack intimacy and the capacity to love want to teach us how to worship. They take the fire of passion out of it. But God said I want to love you as I do My Son! I will never be convinced that God's love for His Son Jesus was cold and heartless. Dead, loveless preachers are killing the spirit of worship.

Why did God write the Song of Solomon? He spoke so that dead religious men who could not define love with God might be enlightened. In this book of love, God could demonstrate His great passion and desires for us.

Go ahead; love God. Let's give Him all our love. Hold nothing back. Let the whole world see. Loving God is not about the world's acceptance; it is not about the world thinking we are okay. Loving God is about God being our hero and our lover in a world that hated Him. We want men to accept us, and they hated Jesus? We want to be seen as civil and normal, and they called Jesus a devil? We cannot love the Father and have the love of the world at the same time. We must choose. Who do we want to think we are fools—the world or God?

Beloved, if we read anything, then carefully read this: the greatest persecution we will ever face when it comes to loving God will be from those within our churches, our families, and our friends. They will resent our ability to see, feel, and know God. We will embarrass them. They will call us mad and unbalanced. They will intimidate us and tell us that we are just trying to be seen. Yep! I sure am—just like a bride who fills up a church with all her family and friends to watch her express and confess her love for her soon-to-be husband. Yep, I want them to see how much I love Him.

I long for the fellowship of the unashamed! I long for the day when the lost are compelled into the church again because of the fame of Jesus and not because of our music or showmanship preachers—that even now, the lost would come to see the glory of a people being loved by the Almighty Lover.

Do we still question all this love stuff, all this emotion, all this talk about affection? Well then, why does God have a bride? Why does God reveal Himself as a Father? Why does God want to be the "LOVER" of my soul? Why do we sing, "Jesus, lover of my soul ...?" Why does God keep all my tears in His bottle? Why has God inscribed me on the palms of His hands? Why does God number my strands of hair? Why did God send His Son? God sent His Son because He is looking for a heart that will reciprocate His love and share in His kingdom.

CHAPTER NOTES:

ABOUT THE AUTHOR

Lee Shipp – Pastor, Author, and International Speaker

With over **40 years of ministry experience**, Pastor **Lee Shipp** is the esteemed **Founder and Senior Pastor** of **First New Testament Church** in Baton Rouge, Louisiana, which he established in **September 1986**. Under his leadership, **by God's Grace and for His Glory**, the church has flourished as a **beacon of faith, scripture, and the power of the Holy Spirit**, shaping countless lives and fostering a thriving Christian community.

Beyond the pulpit, Pastor Shipp is the **President of "A Call to the Heart Ministries"**, a dynamic evangelistic outreach that extends its influence through **radio, television, literature, and international campaigns**. His steadfast **devotion to Christ, scriptural integrity, and reliance on the Holy Ghost** have earned him a reputation as a **sought-after speaker, mentor, and spiritual leader**.

Pastor Shipp's impact reaches far beyond his local congregation. He **ministers to over 300 pastors monthly**, oversees **numerous churches**, and has played a pivotal role in **ordaining ministers** who now serve across the world. His wisdom and leadership are further recognized through his service on **various ministerial boards**, where he continues to shape the future of Christian ministry.

A **prolific writer**, Pastor Shipp has authored **nine books**, with his eagerly anticipated **tenth book set for release in 2025**. His writings, like his ministry, reflect **deep theological insight** and a passion for guiding believers toward a **transformative relationship with Christ**.

At the heart of Pastor Shipp's ministry is his commitment to **evangelism, discipleship, and spiritual leadership**, making him an enduring **voice of truth, inspiration, and faith** in today's world.

Pastor Shipp has been **happily married to Carla for over 39 years**, and together they have **three children who faithfully serve alongside him in ministry**. He resides in **Baton Rouge, Louisiana**.

For more information, visit www.fntchurch.org, https://a-call-to-the-heart-493932.churchcenter.com/home, or call **225-293-2222**. Connect with him on **social media platforms** for updates on his ministry and teachings.

OTHER BOOKS BY PASTOR LEE SHIPP

Why Live This Way When You Don't Have To?

Even Now – The Resurrection of Your Hopes and Dreams

He Never Turned Anyone Away – the Hospitality of Jesus

Satan is Counting On You – Resisting the Lure of Carnal Warfare

Abused by Religion; Healed by the Church

The Cry for His Presence – Praise is the Event that God Responds To

Shame Erased

www.ingramcontent.com/pod-product-compliance
Lightning Source LLC
LaVergne TN
LVHW052028080426
835513LV00018B/2215